NATURAL LANGUAGE PROCESSING
CRASH COURSE
FOR BEGINNERS

THEORY AND APPLICATIONS OF NLP
USING TENSORFLOW AND KERAS

AI PUBLISHING

How to Contact Us

If you have any feedback, please let us know
by sending an email to contact@aipublishing.io.

Your feedback is immensely valued,
and we look forward to hearing from you.
It will be beneficial for us
to improve the quality of our books.

To get the Python codes and materials used in this book,
please click the link below:

www.aipublishing.io/book-nlp-python

The order number is required

About the Publisher

At AI Publishing Company, we have established an international learning platform specifically for young students, beginners, small enterprises, startups, and managers who are new to data sciences and artificial intelligence.

Through our interactive, coherent, and practical books and courses, we help beginners learn skills that are crucial to developing AI and data science projects.

Our courses and books range includes basic introduction courses to language programming and data sciences to advanced courses for machine learning, deep learning, computer vision, big data, and much more, using programming languages like Python, R, and some data science and AI software.

AI Publishing's core focus is to enable our learners to create and try proactive solutions for digital problems by leveraging the power of AI and data sciences to the maximum extent.

Moreover, we offer specialized assistance in the form of our free online content and eBooks, providing up-to-date and useful insight into AI practices and data science subjects, along with eliminating the doubts and misconceptions about AI and programming.

Our experts have cautiously developed our online courses and kept them concise, short, and comprehensive so that you can understand everything clearly and effectively and start practicing the applications right away.

We also offer consultancy and corporate training in AI and data sciences for enterprises so that their staff can navigate through the workflow efficiently.

With AI Publishing, you can always stay closer to the innovative world of AI and data sciences.

If you are eager to learn the A to Z of AI and data sciences but have no clue where to start, AI Publishing is the finest place to go.

Please contact us by email at contact@aipublishing.io.

AI Publishing is Looking for Authors Like You

Interested in becoming an author for AI Publishing?
Please contact us at author@aipublishing.io.

We are working with developers and AI tech professionals just like you, to help them share their insights with the global AI and Data Science lovers. You can share all your knowledge about hot topics in AI and Data Science.

Table of Contents

Preface

§ Book Approach

The book follows a very simple approach. It is divided into 12 chapters. The book is logically divided into two parts. The first 7 chapters explain the theory and basic tasks in NLP, while chapters 8-12 contain some of the most common NLP applications developed in Python.

Chapter 1 introduces the Natural Language Processing (NLP) along with the steps involved in developing an NLP application. Chapter 2 explains the installation steps for the software that we will need to implement various deep learning algorithms in this book. Chapter 2 also contains a crash course on Python.

Chapter 3 explains the basic deep learning concepts that you will use while developing NLP based applications. Chapter 4 is all about text cleaning and manipulation using string and regex functions in Python. Chapter 5 provides a brief introduction to some of the most common preprocessing tasks in NLP, such as tokenization, stemming, lemmatization, etc.

The process of reading text from various sources such as CSV and text files is explained in Chapter 6. This chapter also contains a brief introduction on how to scrape tweets from

Twitter. Chapter 7 explains how to convert text to numbers for statistical algorithms.

The 8th chapter shows how to develop text classification applications such as ham and spam message classification using simple machine learning approaches. The 9th chapter shows how to develop text summarization and topic modeling applications with NLP. The development of sentimental analysis applications with deep learning approaches is explained in chapter 10. The 11th Chapter explains how to develop a text translation application using seq2seq modeling. Finally, the state-of-the-art BERT transformer is explained in Chapter 12.

In each chapter, different types of deep learning and natural language processing techniques have been explained theoretically, followed by practical examples. Each chapter also contains exercises that students can use to evaluate their understanding of the concepts explained in the chapter. The Python notebook for each chapter is provided in the resources. It is advised that instead of copying the code, you write the code yourself. And in case of an error, you match your code with the corresponding Python notebook, find and then correct the error. The datasets used in this book are either downloaded at runtime or are available in the *Resources/ Datasets* folder.

§ Data Science and Natural Language Processing

Data Science and Natural Language Processing are two different but interrelated concepts. Data science refers to the science of extracting and exploring data in order to find patterns that can be used for decision making at different levels. Natural language processing is a subfield of data science which deals with the processing of text data in order to draw out useful information from the data and then use that information to develop various natural language processing applications such as text classification, topic modeling, chatbots, text translation systems, etc.

This book is dedicated to natural language processing and explains how to perform different types of NLP tasks via various machine learning and deep learning algorithms in Python. It is suggested that you use this book for NLP purposes only and not for data science.

§ Who Is This Book For?

This book explains different natural language processing techniques and applications using various NLP libraries for Python. The book is aimed ideally at absolute beginners to deep learning. Though a background in the Python programming language and NLP can help speed up learning, the book contains a crash course on Python programming language in the second chapter. Therefore, the only prerequisite to efficiently using this book is access to a computer with internet. All the codes and datasets have been provided. However, to download data preparation libraries, you will need internet.

§ How to Use This Book?

As I said earlier, natural language techniques and concepts taught in this book have been divided into multiple chapters. To get the best out of this book, I would suggest that you first get your feet wet with the Python programming language, especially the object-oriented programming concepts. To do so, you can take the crash course on Python in chapter 2 of this book. Also, try to read the chapters of this book in order since concepts taught in subsequent chapters are based on previous chapters.

In each chapter, try to first understand the theoretical concepts behind different types of NLP techniques and then try to execute the example code. I would again stress that rather than copying and pasting code, try to write the code yourself, and in case of any error, you can match your code with the source code provided in the book as well as in the Python notebooks in the resources. Finally, try to answer the questions asked in the exercises at the end of each chapter. The solutions to the exercises have been given at the end of the book.

To facilitate the reading process, occasionally, the book presents three types of box-tags in different colors: Requirements, Further Readings, and **Hands-on Time**. Examples of these boxes are shown below.

> **Requirements**
>
> This box lists all requirements needed to be done before proceeding to the next topic. Generally, it works as a checklist to see if everything is ready before a tutorial.

> **Further Readings**
>
> Here, you will be pointed to some external reference or source that will serve as additional content about the specific **Topic** being studied. In general, it consists of packages, documentations, and cheat sheets.

> **Hands-on Time**
>
> Here, you will be pointed to an external file to train and test all the knowledge acquired about a **Tool** that has been studied. Generally, these files are Jupyter notebooks (.ipynb), Python (.py) files, or documents (.pdf).

The box-tag Requirements lists the steps required by the reader after reading one or more topics. Further Readings provides relevant references for specific topics to get to know the additional content of the topics. **Hands-on Time** points to practical tools to start working on the specified topics. Follow the instructions given in the box-tags to get a better understanding of the topics presented in this book.

About the Author

M. Usman Malik holds a Ph.D. in Computer Science from Normandy University, France, with Artificial Intelligence and Machine Learning being his main areas of research. Usman Malik has over 5 years of industry experience in Data Science and has worked with both private and public sector organizations. In his free time, he likes to listen to music and play snooker.

Get in Touch With Us

Feedback from our readers is always welcome.

For general feedback, please send us an email at contact@aipublishing.io and mention the book title in the subject line.

Although we have taken extraordinary care to ensure the accuracy of our content, errors do occur. If you have found an error in this book, we would be grateful if you could report this to us as soon as you can.

If you are interested in becoming an AI Publishing author and if you have expertise in a topic and you are interested in either writing or contributing to a book, please send us an email at author@aipublishing.io.

An Important Note to Our Valued Readers:
Download the Color Images

Our print edition books are available only in black & white at present. However, the digital edition of our books is available in color PDF.

We request you to download the PDF file containing the color images of the screenshots/diagrams used in this book here:

www.aipublishing.io/book-nlp-python

The typesetting and publishing costs for a color edition are prohibitive. These costs would push the final price of each book to $50, which would make the book less accessible for most beginners.

We are a small company, and we are negotiating with major publishers for a reduction in the publishing price. We are hopeful of a positive outcome sometime soon. In the meantime, we request you to help us with your wholehearted support, feedback, and review.

For the present, we have decided to print all of our books in black & white and provide access to the color version in PDF. This is a decision that would benefit the majority of our readers, as most of them are students. This would also allow beginners to afford our books.

Warning

In Python, indentation is very important. Python indentation is a way of telling a Python interpreter that the group of statements belongs to a particular code block. After each loop or if-condition, be sure to pay close attention to the intent.

Example

```python
# Python program showing
# indentation

site = 'aisciences'

if site == 'aisciences':
    print('Logging to www.aisciences.io...')
else:
    print('retype the URL.')
print('All set !')
```

To avoid problems during execution, we advise you to download the codes available on Github by requesting access from the link below. Please have your order number ready for access:

www.aipublishing.io/book-nlp-python

1

What Is Natural Language Processing?

This chapter provides a high-level introduction to natural language processing. The chapter explains what natural language processing is, what some of the most common applications of natural language processing are, and what are the basic approaches used for developing natural language processing applications.

1.1. Understanding Natural Language Processing

Humans interact in natural language. Natural languages contain a lot of information. For example, from the choice of words, the tone and the context of a sentence can be used to exploit the mood, intention, and emotion of a human.

Furthermore, text documents such as books, newspapers, and blogs are full of information that can be exploited to perform various tasks. For humans, it can take a huge amount of time to understand and extract useful information from a text and make decisions based on the information provided in the text.

This is where natural language processing (NLP) comes into play.

Natural language processing is defined as "As a field of artificial intelligence that enables computers to read, understand, and extract meaning from natural languages spoken by humans."

With NLP techniques, computers are not only able to make sense of natural language, but also respond to humans in natural language. Apart from being used for human-computer interaction purposes, NLP techniques are widely used to process huge corporate data, which takes months or even years when processed manually.

For instance, in order to extract information to summarize a book of one thousand pages, a human reader might take weeks of manual effort. With NLP, text summarization can be performed in minutes. Similarly, it is extremely costly to hire manual workers to read through all the user reviews and compile a report containing user opinion about a certain product. With NLP techniques, user opinion can be automatically extracted from text, enabling companies to make organizational decisions.

1.2. NLP Practical Applications

From Microsoft's Cortona to Apple's Siri, NLP has powered a wide variety of applications. This section briefly explains some of the most common applications of NLP.

Sentimental Analysis

NLP is commonly used to perform text sentimental analysis. Public opinion in the form of text, such as tweets, blogs, comments, and reviews about a certain product or entity contains sentiment. Sentiment analysis refers to identifying the sentiment from these texts. Automatic detection of public sentiment regarding a tweet can help companies decide how to improve their products and which product to retain or discard.

Ham and Spam Email Classification

Gmail and other email servers use NLP techniques to differentiate between ham and spam emails with high precision. This is a classic application of text classification where text documents are divided into one of the predefined categories, such as ham or spam.

Speech to Text Conversion

NLP techniques are widely being used to automatically convert speech to text and vice versa. Now, you no longer need to ask someone to write a letter on your behalf while you speak the contents of the letter. Google's Automatic Speech Recognition (ASR) (https://bit.ly/2N6xYSt) model is a classic example of speech to text conversion.

Human-Computer Interaction

Gone are the days when you needed to press keyboard buttons and perform mouse clicks in order to issue commands to machines. NLP has enabled humans to interact with robots via natural language. Robots with the help of NLP are not only able to understand human language but are able to respond to communication in natural language. Sophia (https://bit.ly/2YLprtx) is a classic example of a humanoid robot that interacts with humans via natural language processing.

Powering Personal Assistants

As mentioned earlier, NLP techniques are used to develop personal assistants such as Amazon's Alexa, Apple's Siri, and Microsoft's Cortona. These personal assistants rely on NLP methods in order to understand human queries and respond to them in natural language.

Text Translation

Automatic text translation is one of the most powerful applications of NLP. With text translation techniques, you can translate documents from one language to another with a few mouse clicks. Google translate is one of the most famous examples of text translation using NLP techniques.

Text Summarization

Not everyone has got time to read lengthy texts. Summarizing texts requires time and human effort. With NLP techniques, text documents can be automatically summarized, saving time and human effort and thus cost.

Text Generation

Advanced deep learning-based NLP techniques are now being used for text generation as well. Recently, text generation techniques are being used to generate poetry based on *Game of Thrones* scripts. Text generation techniques are still at inception stages.

1.3. Learning NLP Step by Step Roadmap

Mastering NLP requires time and effort. You cannot claim to be an NLP expert by merely reading through a couple of blogs. This section covers step by step the roadmap to learning NLP.

To be a great NLP expert, you need to follow these steps in order.

1. Know What NLP Is All About

Before you start developing NLP applications, you need to know what you are actually doing. You should know what NLP is all about, why it is useful, and what some of the most important NLP applications are. The first chapter of this book is all about building a foundation in theoretical NLP.

2. Learn a Programming Language

If you wish to be an NLP expert, you have to learn programming. There is no working around this fact. You have to learn to program in order to develop NLP applications. Though you can program natural language applications in any programming language, I would recommend that you learn Python programming language. Python is one of the most commonly used libraries for NLP, with myriads of basic and advanced NLP libraries. In addition, many NLP applications depend on deep learning and machine learning techniques. Again, Python is the language that provides easy- to- use libraries for deep learning and machine learning. In short, learn Python. Chapter 2 contains a crash course for absolute beginners in Python.

3. Start with the Basic Tasks

Start with very basic NLP applications. I would recommend that you should not start developing NLP applications right away. Rather, you should first learn what are the most common and basic NLP tasks. For instance, you should learn how to perform stop word removal, how to divide a sentence into words, and a paragraph into sentences. You should know how to find parts of speech tags for the words in a text, etc. Furthermore, you should be proficient with text cleaning and manipulation techniques. Finally, you should know how to import data from various sources into your application, and how to scrap websites to import data into your applications. Basic NLP tasks have been explained in chapters 4, 5, and 6.

4. Learn How to Represent Text Statistically

As mentioned earlier, most of the advanced NLP techniques involve deep learning and machine learning. Deep learning and machine learning techniques are statistical techniques. To implement these techniques in NLP, you will need to represent text statistically. There are various ways to represent text statistically. Look at chapter 7 for details.

5. Learn Machine Learning and Deep Learning

Once you have learned all the basic NLP concepts, learn machine learning and deep learning concepts, particularly, supervised machine learning algorithms. Among deep learning algorithms, you should know the basic working of a densely connected neural network, a recurrent neural network, particularly LSTM and a convolutional neural network. These concepts are explained in chapter 3.

6. Develop Advanced NLP Applications

Once you are familiar with the basic NLP tasks and have a basic understanding of deep learning and machine learning techniques, you are ready to develop advanced NLP applications. For NLP applications, I would suggest that you first develop machine learning applications like text classification using machine learning algorithms such as Logistic Regression, Random Forest, etc. Once you are comfortable with developing NLP applications with machine learning, you can move toward advanced deep learning-based applications that use various types of neural networks. Part 2 of this book is dedicated to developing machine learning deep learning-based NLP applications.

7. Deploying NLP Application

Advanced NLP based applications are quite similar to machine learning applications. There are several ways to deploy such applications. You can either use dedicated servers containing REST APIs that can be used to call NLP application services. To deploy such applications, you need to learn Python Flask, Docker, or similar web technology. In addition to that, you can also deploy your applications using Amazon Web Services or any other cloud-based deployment platform.

To be an expert NLP practitioner, you need to perform the aforementioned 7 steps in an iterative manner. The more you practice, the better you will get at NLP.

1.4. Major NLP Approaches

Approaches for natural language processing fall into two major categories: rule-based approaches and statistical approaches.

1.4.1. Rule-Based Approaches

Rule-based approaches, as the name suggests, consist of human-defined rules. For instance, a rule-based approach for sentiment classification may contain a rule that if the number of positive words in a tweet is greater than the number of negative words, the tweet can be classified as having an overall positive sentiment.

Rule-based approaches have their own advantages and disadvantages. A major advantage of rule-based approaches is their explainability. In addition, rule-based approaches do not require huge datasets to train. A major downside to rule-based approaches is the fact that these rule-based approaches are not flexible and may not scale to different datasets.

1.4.2. Statistical Approaches

Statistical approaches, as the name suggests, involve statistical algorithms for developing natural language processing techniques. Machine learning and deep learning approaches are prime examples of statistical approaches for NLP. In comparison to rule-based approaches, statistical approaches are more flexible and scalable. A major disadvantage of using statistical approaches is the lack of explainability and the need for huge amounts of dataset in order to train NLP algorithms.

The next chapter describes how to set up an environment to run scripts that are used to perform basic NLP tasks and develop NLP applications.

Further Readings – Python [1]

To learn more about NLP, check these links:

https://bit.ly/3fD8SHd

https://bit.ly/3hNEwDM

https://bit.ly/3OUflnA

For machine learning and deep learning knowledge, refer to these links:

https://bit.ly/2zLXAkE

https://bit.ly/2Y96lyv

Exercises 1

Question 1:

Which of the following is not an application of NLP?

    A. Image Labeling

    B. Poetry Generation

    C. Sentimental Analysis

    D. Email Classification

Question 2:

Which of the following is not an NLP task?

    A. Tokenization

    B. Stop Word Removal

    C. Parts of Speech Tagging

    D. Image Segmentation

Question 3:

Which of the following is not a disadvantage of rule-based approaches for NLP?

    A. Not Flexible

    B. Not Scalable

    C. Require Huge Dataset

    D. None of the Above

2

Environment Setup and Python Crash Course

Various programming languages offer libraries that can be used for NLP tasks. However, you will be using Python programming language for NLP since Python is flexible, easy to learn, and offers the most advanced NLP and machine learning libraries.

In this chapter, you will see how to set up the Python environment needed to run various natural language processing libraries. The chapter also contains a crash Python course for absolute beginners in Python. Finally, the different machine learning and natural language processing libraries that we are going to study in this book have been discussed. The chapter ends with a simple exercise.

2.1. Environment Setup

2.1.1. Windows Setup

The time has come to install Python on Windows using an IDE. In fact, we will use Anaconda throughout this book right from installing the Python to writing multi-threaded codes in the coming lectures. Now, let us get going with the installation.

This section explains how you can download and install Anaconda on Windows.

To download and install Anaconda, follow these steps.

1. Open the following URL in your browser.

    https://www.anaconda.com/distribution/

2. The browser will take you to the following webpage. Select the latest version of Python (3.7 at the time of writing this book). Now, click the *Download* button to download the executable file. Depending upon the speed of your internet, the file will download within 2–3 minutes.

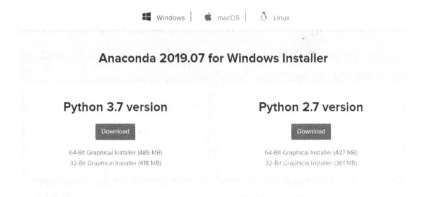

3. Run the executable file after the download is complete. You will most likely find the downloaded file in your download folder. The name of the file should be similar to "Anaconda3-5.1.0-Windows-x86_64." The installation wizard will open when you run the file, as shown in the following figure. Click the *Next* button.

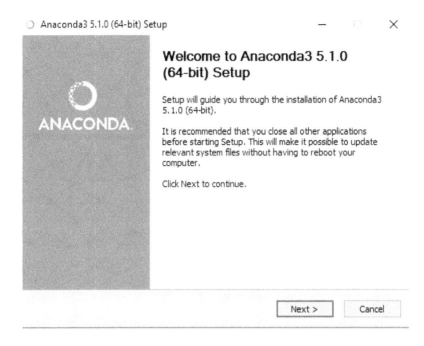

4. Now click *I Agree* on the **License Agreement** dialog, as shown in the following screenshot.

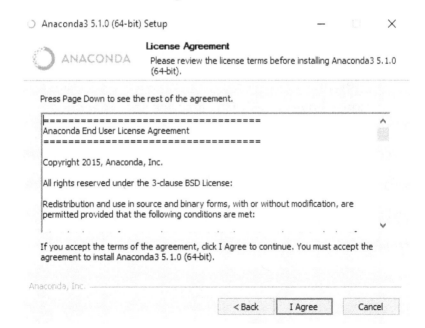

5. Check the *Just Me* radio button from the **Select Installation Type** dialogue box. Click the *Next* button to continue.

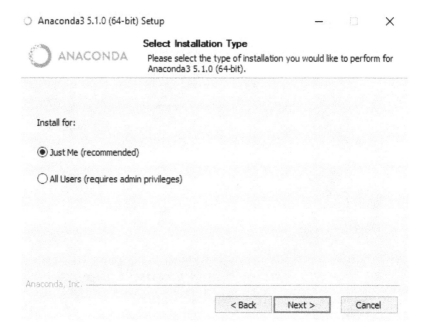

6. Now, the **Choose Install Location** dialog will be displayed. Change the directory if you want, but the default is preferred. The installation folder should at least have 3 GB of free space for Anaconda. Click the *Next* button.

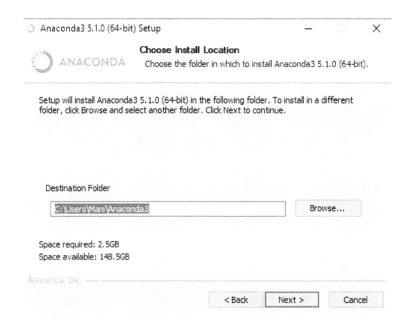

7. Go for the second option, *Register Anaconda as my default Python 3.7* in the **Advanced Installation Options** dialogue box. Click the *Install* button to start the installation, which can take some time to complete.

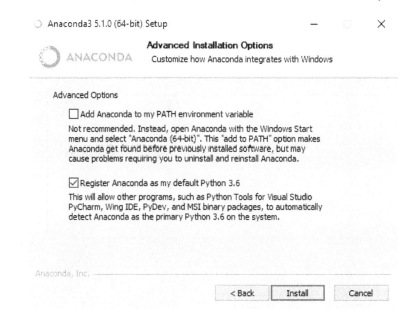

8. Click *Next* once the installation is complete.

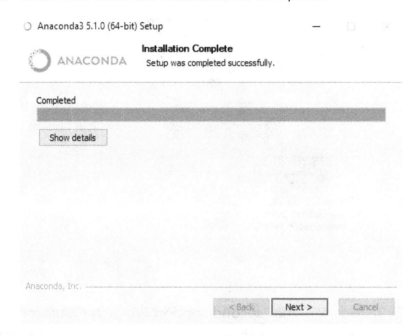

9. Click *Skip* on the **Microsoft Visual Studio Code Installation** dialog box.

10. You have successfully installed Anaconda on your Windows. Excellent job. The next step is to uncheck both checkboxes on the dialog box. Now, click on the Finish button.

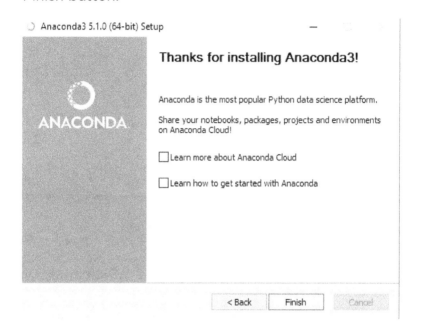

2.1.2. Mac Setup

Anaconda's installation process is almost the same for Mac. It may differ graphically, but you will follow the same steps you followed for Windows. The only difference is that you have to download the executable file, which is compatible with the Mac operating system.

This section explains how you can download and install Anaconda on Mac.

Follow these steps to download and install Anaconda.

1. Open the following URL in your browser.

   https://www.anaconda.com/distribution/

2. The browser will take you to the following webpage. Select the latest version of Python for Mac. (3.7 at the time of writing this book). Now, click the *Download* button to download the executable file. Depending upon the speed of your internet, the file will download within 2–3 minutes.

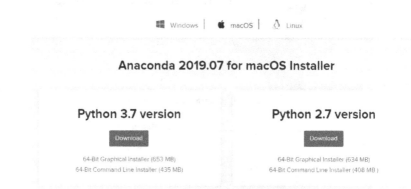

3. Run the executable file after the download is complete. You will most likely find the downloaded file in your download folder. The name of the file should be similar to "Anaconda3-5.1.0-Windows-x86_64." The installation wizard will open when you run the file, as shown in the following figure. Click the *Continue* button.

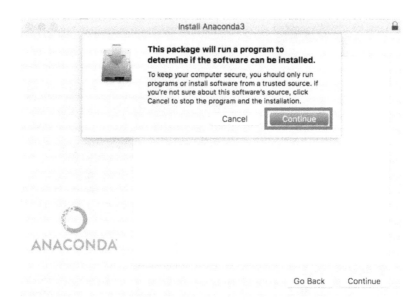

4. Now click *Continue* on the **Welcome to Anaconda 3 Installer** window, as shown in the following screenshot.

5. The **Important Information** dialog will pop up. Simply, click *Continue* to go with the default version that is Anaconda 3.

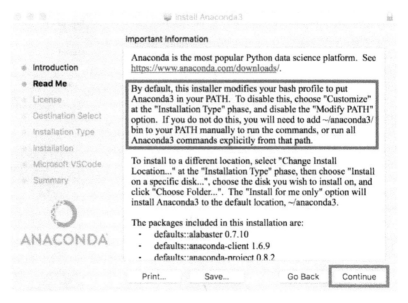

6. Click *Continue* on the **Software License Agreement** Dialog.

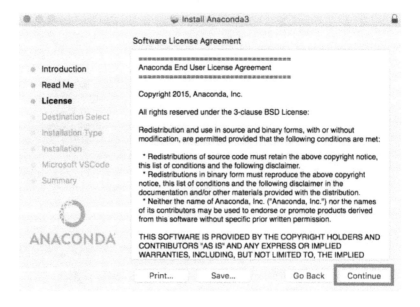

7. It is mandatory to read the license agreement and click the *Agree* button before you can click the *Continue* button again.

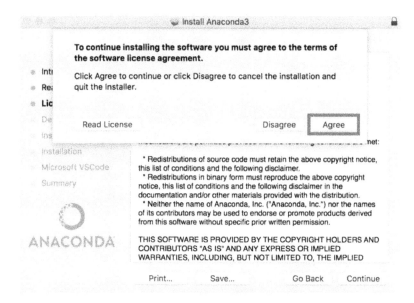

8. Simply click *Install* on the next window that appears.

The system will prompt you to give your password. Use the same password you use to login to your Mac computer. Now, click on *Install Software*.

9. Click *Continue* on the next window. You also have the option to install Microsoft VSCode at this point.

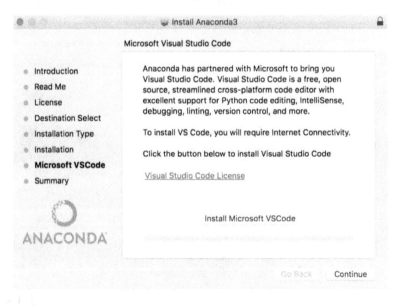

The next screen will display the message that the installation has completed successfully. Click on the *Close* button to close the installer.

There you have it. You have successfully installed Anaconda on your Mac computer. Now, you can write Python code in Jupyter and Spyder the same way you wrote it in Windows.

2.1.3. Linux Setup

We have used Python's graphical installers for installation on Windows and Mac. However, we will use the command line to install Python on Ubuntu or Linux. Linux is also more resource-friendly, and the installation of software is particularly easy as well.

Follow these steps to install Anaconda on Linux (Ubuntu distribution).

1.   Go to the following link to copy the installer bash script from the latest available version.

https://www.anaconda.com/distribution/

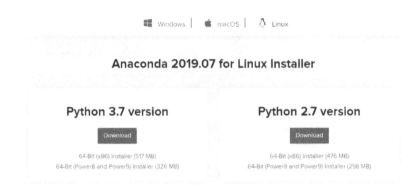

2. The second step is to download the installer bash script. Log into your Linux computer and open your terminal. Now, go to /temp directory and download the bash you downloaded from Anaconda's home page using curl.

```
$ cd / tmp

$ curl -o https://repo.anaconda.com.archive/Anaconda3-5.2.0-
Linux-x86_64.sh
```

3. You should also use the cryptographic hash verification through SHA-256 checksum to verify the integrity of the installer.

```
$ sha256sum Anaconda3-5.2.0-Linux-x86_64.sh
```

You will get the following output.

```
f53738b0cd3bb96f5b1bac488e5528df9906be2480fe61df40e0e0d19e3d48
Anaconda3-5.2.0-Linux-x86_64.sh
```

4. The fourth step is to run the Anaconda Script, as shown in the following figure.

```
$ bash Anaconda3-5.2.0-Linux-x86_64.sh
```

The command line will produce the following output. You will be asked to review the license agreement. Keep on pressing *Enter* until you reach the end.

```
Output

Welcome to Anaconda3 5.2.0

In order to continue the installation process, please review
the license agreement.
Please, press Enter to continue
>>>
...
Do you approve the license terms? [yes|No]
```

Type *Yes* when you get to the bottom of the License Agreement.

5. The installer will ask you to choose the installation location after you agree to the license agreement. Simply press *Enter* to choose the default location. You can also specify a different location if you want.

```
Output

Anaconda3 will now be installed on this location:
/home/tola/anaconda3

- Press ENTER to confirm the location
- Press CTRL-C to abort the installation
- Or specify a different location below

[/home/tola/anaconda3] >>>
```

The installation will proceed once you press *Enter*. Once again, you have to be patient as the installation process takes some time to complete.

6. You will receive the following result when the installation is complete. If you wish to use **conda** command, type *Yes*.

```
Output
...
Installation finished.
Do you wish the installer to prepend Anaconda3 install
location to path in your /home/tola/.bashrc? [yes|no]
[no]>>>
```

At this point, you will also have the option to download the Visual Studio Code. Type *yes* or *no* to install or decline, respectively.

7. Use the following command to activate your brand-new installation of Anaconda3.

```
$ source `/.bashrc
```

8. You can also test the installation using the conda command.

```
$ conda list
```

Congratulations. You have successfully installed Anaconda on your Linux system.

2.1.4. Using Google Colab Cloud Environment

In addition to local Python environments such as Anaconda, you can run deep learning applications on Google Colab as well, which is Google's platform for deep learning with GPU support. All the codes in this book have been run using Google Colab. Therefore, I would suggest that you use Google Colab too.

To run deep learning applications via Google Colab, all you need is a Google/Gmail account. Once you have a Google/Gmail account, you can simply go to:

https://colab.research.google.com/

Next, click on File -> New notebook, as shown in the following screenshot.

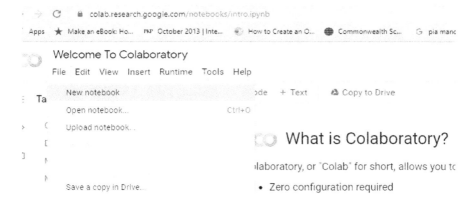

Next, to run your code using GPU, from the top menu, select Runtime -> Change runtime type as shown in the following screenshot:

Runtime   Tools   Help   Last edited on M

Run all   Ctrl+F9

Run before   Ctrl+F8

Run the focused cell   Ctrl+Enter

Run selection   Ctrl+Shift+Enter

Run after   Ctrl+F10

Factory reset runtime

Change runtime type

Manage sessions

You should see the following window. Here, from the dropdown list, select GPU, and click the *Save* button.

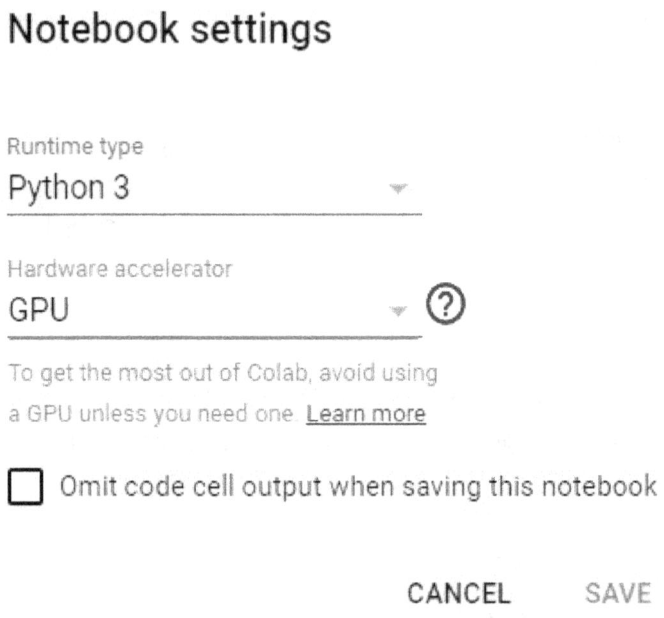

Notebook settings

Runtime type

Python 3 ▾

Hardware accelerator

GPU ▾ ⑦

To get the most out of Colab, avoid using
a GPU unless you need one. Learn more

☐ Omit code cell output when saving this notebook

CANCEL   SAVE

To make sure you are running the latest version of TensorFlow, execute the following script in the Google Colab notebook cell. The following script will update your TensorFlow version.

```
pip install --upgrade tensorflow
```

To check if you are really running TensorFlow version > 2.0, execute the following script.

```
1.    import tensorflow as tf
2.    print(tf.__version__)
```

With Google cloud, you can import the datasets from your Google drive. Execute the following script. And click on the link that appears as shown below:

```
from google.colab import drive
drive.mount('/gdrive')

Go to this URL in a browser: https://accounts.google.com/o/oauth2/auth

Enter your authorization code:
```

You will be prompted to allow Google Colab to access your Google drive. Click *Allow* button as shown below:

G Sign in with Google

Google Drive File Stream wants to access your Google Account

engr.m.usmanmalik@gmail.com

This will allow Google Drive File Stream **to:**

- See, edit, create, and delete all of your Google Drive files ⓘ

- View the photos, videos and albums in your Google Photos ⓘ

- View Google people information such as profiles and contacts ⓘ

- See, edit, create, and delete any of your Google Drive documents ⓘ

Make sure you trust Google Drive File Stream

You may be sharing sensitive info with this site or app. Learn about how Google Drive File Stream will handle your data by reviewing its terms of service and privacy policies. You can always see or remove access in your Google Account.

Learn about the risks

Cancel   **Allow**

You will see a link appear, as shown in the following image. (The link has been blinded here.)

Google

Sign in

Please copy this code, switch to your application and paste it there:

cIjiqzw

Copy the link. Next, paste it in the empty field in the Google Colab cell, as shown below:

```
from google.colab import drive
drive.mount('/gdrive')

Go to this URL in a browser: https://accounts.google.com/o/oauth2/auth

Enter your authorization code:
```

This way, you can import datasets from your Google drive to your Google Colab environment.

2.2. Python Crash Course

If you are familiar with the basic concepts of the Python programming language, you can skip this section. For those who are absolute beginners to Python, this section provides a very brief overview of some of the most basic concepts of Python. Python is a very vast programming language, and this section is by no means a substitute for a complete Python book. However, if you want to see how various operations and commands are executed in Python, you are welcome to follow along the rest of this section.

2.2.1. Writing Your First Program

You have already installed Python on your computer and established a unique environment in the form of Anaconda. Now, it is time to write your first program, that is the Hello World!

In order to write a program in Anaconda, you have to launch Anaconda Navigator. Search "Anaconda Navigator" in your Windows Search Box. Now, click on the Anaconda Navigator application icon as shown in the following figure.

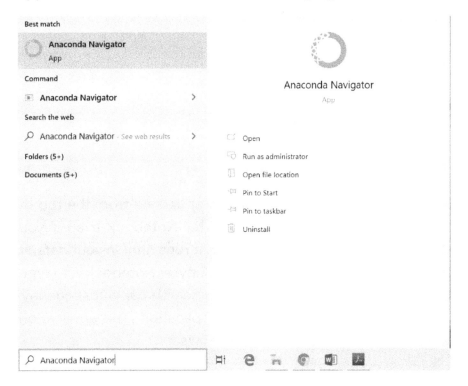

Once you click on the application, Anaconda's Dashboard will open. The dashboard offers you a myriad of tools to write your code. We will use the *Jupyter Notebook*, the most popular of these tools, to write and explain the code throughout this book.

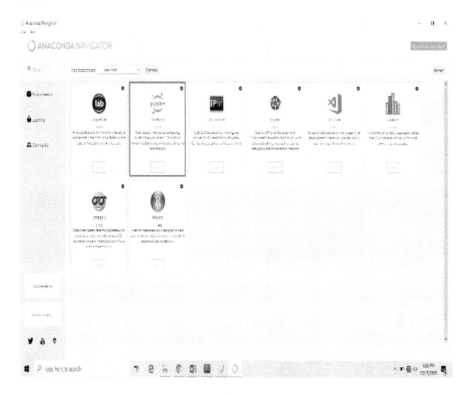

The Jupyter Notebook is available at second from the top of the dashboard. You can use Jupyter Notebook even if you don't have access to the internet as it runs right in your default browser. Another method to open Jupyter Notebook is to type *Jupyter Notebook* in the Window's search bar. Subsequently, click on the Jupyter Notebook application. The application will open in the new tab of your browser.

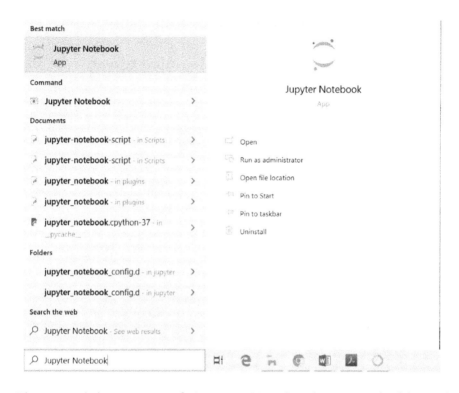

The top right corner of Jupyter Notebook's own dashboard houses a *New* button, which you have to click to open a new document. A dropdown containing several options will appear. Click on *Python 3*.

A new Python notebook will appear for you to write your programs. It looks as follows.

Jupyter Notebook consists of cells, as evident from the above image, making its layout very simple and straightforward. You will write your code inside these cells. Let us write our first ever Python program in Jupyter Notebook.

1.3.1. Writing Your First Program

```
In [1]: print("Welcome to Data Visualization with Python")

        Welcome to Data Visualization with Python
```

The above script basically prints a string value in the output using the **print()** method. The **print()** method is used to print on the console, any string passed to it. If you see the following output, you have successfully run your first Python program.

Output:

```
Welcome to Data Visualization with Python
```

Let's now explore some of the other important Python concepts starting with Variables and Data Types.

> **Requirements – Anaconda, Jupyter, and Matplotlib**
> - All the scripts in this book have been executed via Jupyter notebook. Therefore, you should have Jupyter notebook installed.

> **Hands-on Time – Source Codes**
> All IPython notebooks for the source code of all the scripts in this chapter can be found in Resources/Chapter 2.ipynb. I would suggest that you write all the code in this chapter yourself and see if you can get the same output as mentioned in this Chapter.

2.2.2. Python Variables and Data Types

Data types in a programming language refers to the type of data that the language is capable of processing. The following are the major data types supported by Python.

a. Strings

b. Integers

c. Floating Point Numbers

d. Booleans

e. Lists

f. Tuples

g. Dictionaries

A variable is an alias for the memory address where actual data is stored. The data or the values stored at a memory address can be accessed and updated via the variable name. Unlike other programming languages like C++, Java, and C#, Python is loosely typed, which means that you don't have to specify the data type while creating a variable. Rather, the type of data is evaluated at runtime.

The following example demonstrates how to create different data types and how to store them in their corresponding variables. The script also prints the type of the variables via the **type()** function.

Script 1:

```
1.  # A string Variable
2.  first_name = "Joseph"
3.  print(type(first_name))
4.
5.  # An Integer Variable
6.  age = 20
7.  print(type(age))
8.
9.  # A floating point variable
10. weight = 70.35
11. print(type(weight))
12.
13. # A boolean variable
14. married = False
15. print(type(married))
16.
17. #List
18. cars = ["Honda", "Toyota", "Suzuki"]
19. print(type(cars))
20.
21. #Tuples
22. days = ("Sunday", "Monday", "Tuesday", "Wednesday",
    "Thursday", "Friday", "Saturday")
23. print(type(days))
24.
25. #Dictionaries
26. days2 = {1:"Sunday", 2:"Monday", 3:"Tuesday",
    4:"Wednesday", 5:"Thursday", 6:"Friday", 7:"Saturday"}
27. print(type(days2))
```

Output:

```
<class 'str'>
<class 'int'>
<class 'float'>
<class 'bool'>
<class 'list'>
<class 'tuple'>
<class 'dict'>
```

2.2.3. Python Operators

Python programming language contains the following types of operators:

a. Arithmetic Operators

b. Logical Operators

c. Comparison Operators

d. Assignment Operators

e. Membership Operators

Let's briefly review each of these types of operators.

Arithmetic Operators

Arithmetic operators are used to perform arithmetic operations in Python. The following table summarizes the arithmetic operators supported by Python. Suppose X = 20 and Y = 10.

Operator Name	Symbol	Functionality	Example
Addition	+	Adds the operands on either side	X+ Y= 30
Subtraction	-	Subtracts the operands on either side	X -Y= 10
Multiplication	*	Multiplies the operands on either side	X * Y= 200

Division	/	Divides the operand on the left by the one on right	X / Y= 2.0
Modulus	%	Divides the operand on the left by the one on right and returns remainder	X % Y= 0
Exponent	**	Takes exponent of the operand on the left to the power of right	X ** Y = $1024 \times e^{10}$

Here is an example of arithmetic operators with output:

Script 2:

```
1. X = 20
2. Y = 10
3. print(X + Y)
4. print(X - Y)
5. print(X * Y)
6. print(X / Y)
7. print(X ** Y)
```

Output:

```
30
10
200
2.0
10240000000000
```

Logical Operators

Logical operators are used to perform logical **AND, OR**, and **NOT** operations in Python. The following table summarizes the logical operators. Here **X** is **True**, and **Y** is **False**.

Operator	Symbol	Functionality	Example
Logical AND	and	The condition becomes true if both the operands are true.	(X and Y) = False

| Logical OR | or | The condition becomes true if any of the two operands are true. | (X or Y) = True |
| Logical NOT | not | Used to reverse the logical state of its operand. | not(X and Y) =True |

Here is an example that explains the usage of Python logical operators.

Script 3:

```
1.  X = True
2.  Y = False
3.  print(X and Y)
4.  print(X or Y)
5.  print(not(X and Y))
```

Output:

```
1.  False
2.  True
3.  True
```

Comparison Operators

Comparison operators, as the name suggests, are used to compare two or more than two operands. Depending upon the relation between the operands, comparison operators return Boolean values. The following table summarizes comparison operators in Python. Here X is 20, and Y is 35.

Operator	Symbol	Description	Example
Equality	==	If the values of both the operands are equal, then the condition returns true.	(X == Y) = false
Inequality	!=	If the values of both the operands are not equal, then the condition returns true.	(X = Y) = true

Greater than	>	If the value of the left operand is greater than the right one, then the condition returns true.	(X> Y) = False
Smaller than	<	Returns true if value of the left operand is smaller than the right one	(X< Y) = True
Greater than or equal to	>=	If the value of the left operand is greater than or equal to the right one, then the condition returns true.	(X > =Y) = False
Smaller than or equal to	<=	If the value of the left operand is smaller than or equal to the right one, then the condition returns true.	(X<= Y) = True

The comparison operators have been demonstrated in action in the following example:

Script 4:

```
1.  X = 20
2.  Y = 35
3.
4.  print(X == Y)
5.  print(X != Y)
6.  print(X > Y)
7.  print(X < Y)
8.  print(X >= Y)
9.  print(X <= Y)
```

Output:

```
False
True
False
True
False
True
```

Assignment Operators

Assignment operators are used to assign values to variables. The following table summarizes the assignment operators. Here, X is 20, and Y is equal to 10.

Operator	Symbol	Description	Example
Assignment	=	Used to assign value of the right operand to the one on the left.	R = X+ Y assigns 30 to R
Add and assign	+=	Adds the operands on either side and assigns the result to the left operand	X += Y assigns 30 to X
Subtract and assign	-=	Subtracts the operands on either side and assigns the result to the left operand	X -= Y assigns 10 to X
Multiply and Assign	*=	Multiplies the operands on either side and assigns the result to the left operand	X *= Y assigns 200 to X
Divide and Assign	/=	Divides the operands on the left by the right and assigns the result to the left operand	X/= Y assigns 2 to X
Take modulus and assign	%=	Divides the operands on the left by the right and assigns the remainder to the left operand	X %= Y assigns 0 to X
Take exponent and assign	**=	Takes exponent of the operand on the left to the power of right and assign the remainder to the left operand	X **= Y assigns 1024 x e^{10} to X

Take a look at script 6 to see Python assignment operators in action.

Script 5:

```
1.  X = 20; Y = 10
2.  R = X + Y
3.  print(R)
4.
5.  X = 20;
6.  Y = 10
7.  X += Y
8.  print(X)
9.
10. X = 20;
11. Y = 10
12. X -= Y
13. print(X)
14.
15. X = 20;
16. Y = 10
17. X *= Y
18. print(X)
19.
20. X = 20;
21. Y = 10
22. X /= Y
23. print(X)
24.
25. X = 20;
26. Y = 10
27. X %= Y
28. print(X)
29.
30. X = 20;
31. Y = 10
32. X **= Y
33. print(X)
```

Output:

```
30
30
10
200
2.0
0
10240000000000
```

Membership Operators

Membership operators are used to find if an item is a member of a collection of items or not. There are two types of membership operators: The **in** operator and the **not in** operator. The following script shows the **in** operator in action.

Script 6:

```
1.  days = ("Sunday", "Monday", "Tuesday", "Wednesday",
        "Thursday", "Friday", "Saturday")
2.  print('Sunday' in days)
```

Output:

```
True
```

And here is an example of the **not in** operator.

Script 7:

```
1.  days = ("Sunday", "Monday", "Tuesday", "Wednesday",
        "Thursday", "Friday", "Saturday")
2.  print('Xunday' not in days)
```

Output:

```
True
```

2.2.4. Conditional Statements

Conditional statements in Python are used to implement conditional logic in Python. Conditional statements help you decide whether to execute a certain code block or not. There are three main types of conditional statements in Python:

a. If statement

b. If-else statement

c. If-elif statement

IF Statement

If you have to check for a single condition and you do not concern about the alternate condition, you can use the **if** statement. For instance, if you want to check if 10 is greater than 5 and based on that you want to print a statement, you can use the if statement. The condition evaluated by the **if** statement returns a Boolean value. If the condition evaluated by the **if** statement is true, the code block that follows the **if** statement executes. It is important to mention that in Python, a new code block starts at a new line with on tab indented from the left when compared with the outer block.

Here, in the following example, the condition 10 > 5 is evaluated, which returns true. Hence, the code block that follows the **if** statement executes, and a message is printed on the console.

Script 8:

```
1.  # The if statement
2.
3.  if 10 > 5:
4.      print("Ten is greater than 10")
```

Output:

```
Ten is greater than 10
```

IF-Else Statement

The **If-else** statement comes handy when you want to execute an alternate piece of code in case the condition for the if statement returns false. For instance, in the following example, the condition 5 < 10 will return false. Hence, the code block that follows the **else** statement will execute.

Script 9:

```
1.  # if-else statement
2.
3.  if  5 > 10:
4.      print("5 is greater than 10")
5.  else:
6.      print("10 is greater than 5")
```

Output:

```
10 is greater than 5
```

IF-Elif Statement

The **if-elif** statement comes handy when you have to evaluate multiple conditions. For instance, in the following example, we first check if 5 > 10, which evaluates to false. Next, an **elif** statement evaluates the condition 8 < 4, which also returns false. Hence, the code block that follows the last **else** statement executes.

Script 10:

```
1.  #if-elif and else
2.
3.  if  5 > 10:
4.      print("5 is greater than 10")
5.  elif 8 < 4:
6.      print("8 is smaller than 4")
7.  else:
8.      print("5 is not greater than 10 and 8 is not smaller
    than 4")
```

Output:

```
5 is not greater than 10 and 8 is not smaller than 4
```

2.2.5. Iteration Statements

Iteration statements, also known as loops, are used to iteratively execute a certain piece of code. There are two main types of iteration statements in Python.

    a. For loop

    b. While Loop

For Loop

The **for loop** is used to iteratively execute a piece of code for a certain number of times. You should use **for loop** when you exactly know the number of iterations or repetitions for which you want to run your code. A **for loop** iterates over a collection of items. In the following example, we create a collection of five integers using the **range()** method. Next, a **for loop** iterates five times and prints each integer in the collection.

Script 11:

```
1. items = range(5)
2. for item in items:
3.     print(item)
```

Output:

```
0
1
2
3
4
```

While Loop

The **while loop** keeps executing a certain piece of code unless the evaluation condition becomes false. For instance, the **while loop** in the following script keeps executing unless variable c becomes greater than 10.

Script 12:

```
1. c = 0
2. while c < 10:
3.     print(c)
4.     c = c +1
```

Output:

```
0
1
2
3
4
5
6
7
8
9
```

2.2.6. Functions

In any programming language, functions are used to implement that piece of code that is required to be executed several times at different locations in the code. In such cases, instead of writing long pieces of codes again and again, you can simply define a function that contains the piece of code, and then you can call the function wherever you want in the code.

To create a function in Python, the def keyword is used, followed by the name of the function and opening and closing parenthesis.

Once a function is defined, you have to call it in order to execute the code inside a function body. To call a function, you simply have to specify the name of the function, followed by opening and closing parenthesis. In the following script, we create a function named **myfunc,** which prints a simple statement on the console using **print()** method.

Script 13:

```
1.  def myfunc():
2.      print("This is a simple function")
3.
4.  ### function call
5.  myfunc()
```

Output:

```
This is a simple function
```

You can also pass values to a function. The values are passed inside the parenthesis of the function call. However, you must specify the parameter name in the function definition, too. In the following script, we define a function named **myfuncparam()**. The function accepts one parameter, i.e.,

num. The value passed in the parenthesis of the function call will be stored in this **num** variable and will be printed by the **print()**method inside the **myfuncparam()** method.

Script 14:

```
1.  def myfuncparam(num):
2.      print("This is a function with parameter value: "+num)
3.
4.  ### function call
5.  myfuncparam("Parameter 1")
```

Output:

```
This is a function with parameter value:Parameter 1
```

Finally, a function can also return values to the function call. To do so, you simply have to use the return keyword, followed by the value that you want to return. In the following script, the **myreturnfunc()** function returns a string value to the calling function.

Script 15:

```
1.  def myreturnfunc():
2.      return "This function returns a value"
3.
4.  val = myreturnfunc()
5.  print(val)
```

Output:

```
This function returns a value
```

2.2.7. Objects and Classes

Python supports object-oriented programming (OOP). In OOP, any entity that can perform some function and have some attributes is implemented in the form of an object.

For instance, a car can be implemented as an object since a car has some attributes such as price, color, and model, and it can perform some functions such as drive car, change gear, stop car, etc.

Similarly, a fruit can also be implemented as an object since a fruit has a price and name, and you can eat a fruit, grow a fruit, and perform functions with a fruit.

To create an object, you first have to define a class. For instance, in the following example, a class **Fruit** has been defined. The class has two attributes **name** and **price**, and one method **eat_ fruit()**. Next, we create an object **f** of class Fruit and then call the **eat_fruit()** method from the **f** object. We also access the **name** and **price** attributes of the **f** object and print them on the console.

Script 16:

```
1.  class Fruit:
2.
3.      name = "apple"
4.      price = 10
5.
6.      def eat_fruit(self):
7.          print("Fruit has been eaten")
8.
9.
10. f = Fruit()
11. f.eat_fruit()
12. print(f.name)
13. print(f.price)
```

Output:

```
Fruit has been eaten
apple
10
```

A class in Python can have a special method called a constructor. The name of the constructor method in Python is **__init__().** The constructor is called whenever an object of a class is created. Look at the following example to see the constructor in action.

Script 17:

```
1.  class Fruit:
2.
3.      name = "apple"
4.      price = 10
5.
6.      def __init__(self, fruit_name, fruit_price):
7.          Fruit.name = fruit_name
8.          Fruit.price = fruit_price
9.
10.     def eat_fruit(self):
11.         print("Fruit has been eaten")
12.
13.
14. f = Fruit("Orange", 15)
15. f.eat_fruit()
16. print(f.name)
17. print(f.price)
```

Output:

```
Fruit has been eaten
Orange
15
```

Further Readings – Python [1]

To study more about Python, please check Python 3 Official Documentation. Get used to searching and reading this documentation. It is a great resource.

2.3. Natural Language Processing Libraries

Owing to the growing importance of natural language processing, several Python libraries have been developed. Some of these libraries have been briefly reviewed in this section.

2.3.1. NLTK

NLTK stands for Natural Language Toolkit (NLTK) and is one of the oldest and most commonly used natural language processing libraries in Python.

In addition to providing basic NLP functionalities such as tokenization, POS-tagging, stop word removal and chunking, etc., the NLTK library can also be used for text classification, sentimental analysis, and other advanced tasks.

To know more about NLTK, check this link:

https://www.nltk.org/

2.3.2. Gensim

Genism is another high-level natural language processing library that can be used for common NLP tasks such as named entity recognition, tokenization. In addition, Gensim is also used to create word embedding vectors.

To study more about Gensim, check this link:

https://www.machinelearningplus.com/nlp/gensim-tutorial/

2.3.3. SpaCy

SpaCy is one of the most advanced natural language libraries in Python. With SpaCy, you can perform many advanced tasks such as sentimental analysis, text summarization, semantic similarity, and so on. SpaCy is the industrial standard library for NLP. To study more about SpaCy, check this link: https:// spacy.io/

In addition to pure NLP libraries such as NLTK, Gensim, and SpaCy, some machine learning and deep learning libraries like TensorFlow, Keras, and Scikit Learn also offer natural language processing.

2.3.4. TensorFlow

TensorFlow is one of the most commonly used libraries for deep learning. TensorFlow has been developed by Google and offers an easy to use API for the development of various deep learning models.

TensorFlow is consistently being updated, and at the time of writing of this book, TensorFlow 2 is the latest major release. With TensorFlow, you can not only easily develop deep learning applications but also deploy them with ease, owing to the deployment functionalities of TensorFlow.

To study more about TensorFlow, check this link:

https://www.tensorflow.org/

2.3.5. Keras

Keras is a high-level TensorFlow library that implements complex TensorFlow functionalities under the hood. If you are new to deep learning, Keras is the one deep learning library that you should start for developing a deep learning library. As a matter of fact, Keras has been adopted as the official deep learning library for TensorFlow 2.0, and now all the TensorFlow applications use Keras abstractions for training deep learning models.

To study more about Keras, check this link: https://keras.io/

2.3.6. NumPy

NumPy is one of the most routinely used libraries for numeric and scientific computing. NumPy is extremely fast and contains support for multiple mathematical domains such as linear algebra, geometry, etc. It is extremely important to learn NumPy in case you plan to make a career in data science and data preparation.

To know more about NumPy, check this link:

https://numpy.org/

2.3.7. Scikit Learn

Scikit Learn, also called sklearn, is an extremely useful library for machine learning in Python. Sklearn contains many built-in modules that can be used to perform data preparation tasks such as feature engineering, feature scaling, outlier detection, discretization, etc. You will be using Sklearn a lot in this book. Therefore, it can be a good idea to study sklearn before you start coding using this book.

To study more about Scikit Learn, check this link:

https://scikit-learn.org/stable/

2.3.8. Matplotlib

Before you actually apply NLP techniques on the data, you should know how the data looks like, what is the distribution of a certain variable, etc. Matplotlib is the de facto standard for static data visualization in Python.

To study more about Matplotlib, check this link:

https://matplotlib.org/

2.3.9. Seaborn

Seaborn library is built on top of the Matplotlib library and contains all the plotting capabilities of Matplotlib. However, with Seaborn, you can plot much more pleasing and aesthetic graphs with the help of Seaborn default styles and color palettes. To study more about Seaborn, check this link: https://seaborn.pydata.org/

2.3.10. Pandas

Pandas library, like Seaborn, is based on the Matplotlib library and offers utilities that can be used to plot different types of static plots in a single line of codes. With Pandas, you can import data in various formats such as CSV (Comma Separated View) and TSV (Tab Separated View), and you can plot a variety of data visualizations via these data sources. To know more about Seaborn, check this link: https://pandas.pydata.org/

> ### Hands-on Time – Exercise
>
> Now, it is your turn. Follow the instructions in **the exercises** to check your understanding of the basic Python concepts. The answers to these questions are given at the end of the book.

Exercise 2.1

Question 1

Which iteration should be used when you want to repeatedly execute a code specific number of times?

A. For Loop
B. While Loop
C. Both A and B
D. None of the above

Question 2

What is the maximum number of values that a function can return in Python?

A. Single Value
B. Double Value
C. More than two values
D. None

Question 3

Which of the following membership operators are supported by Python?

A. In
B. Out
C. Not In
D. Both A and C

Exercise 2.2

Print the table of integer 9 using a while loop:

3

Introduction to Deep Learning

3.1. What Is a Neural Network?

In its simplest form, a neural network is a network of mathematical functions that map inputs to corresponding outputs. A neural network is capable of learning non-linear boundaries between different types of datasets. Neural networks can be used to solve classification, regression, and clustering tasks.

Since most of the advanced natural language processing applications NLP tasks involve classification, regression, and clustering, the role of deep learning or neural networks has increased many-folds for NLP. Specialized neural networks such as RNN and LSTM have been developed for NLP tasks.

In this chapter, you will briefly study the theory behind the different types of neural networks. You will study a simply densely connected neural network (DNN), a convolutional neural network (CNN), a recurrent neural network (RNN), and LSTM (which is a type of recurrent neural network). In chapters

9, 10, and 11, you will see the practical implementation of deep neural networks for natural language processing.

3.1.1. DNN Neural Network with One Output

In this section, you will implement a densely connected neural network with a single output from scratch. You will be learning how to find a non-linear boundary to separate two classes. Let's define our dataset:

Script 1:

```
1.  from sklearn import datasets
2.  import numpy as np
3.  import matplotlib.pyplot as plt
4.  %matplotlib inline
5.
6.  np.random.seed(0)
7.  X, y = datasets.make_moons(100, noise=0.10)
8.  x1 = X[:,0]
9.  x2 = X[:,1]
10.
11. plt.figure(figsize=(10,7))
12. plt.scatter(x1, x2, c= y, cmap=plt.cm.coolwarm)
```

Output:

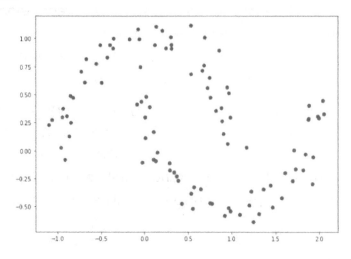

Our dataset has 100 records with two features and one output. You will need to reshape the output so that it has the same structure as the input features:

Script 2:

```
y = y.reshape(y.shape[0],1)
```

We can now check the shape of our input features and output labels:

Script 3:

```
1.      print(X.shape)
2.      print(y.shape)
```

Output:

```
(100, 2)
(100, 1)
```

Before we move forward, let's define the structure of our neural network. Our neural network will look like this:

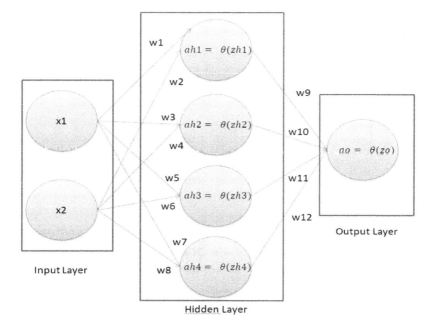

In a neural network, we have an input layer, one or multiple hidden layers, and an output layer. In our neural network, we have two nodes in the input layer (since there are two features in the input), one hidden layer with four nodes, and one output layer with one node since we are doing binary classification. The number of hidden layers and the number of neurons per hidden layer depend upon you.

In the above neural network, the x1 and x2 are the input features, and the ao is the output of the network. Here, the only thing we can control is the weights w1, w2, w3, ... w12. The idea is to find the values of weights, for which the difference between the predicted output ao in this case and the actual output (labels) is minimum.

A neural network works in two steps:

1. Feed Forward
2. Back Propagation

I will explain both these steps in the context of our neural network.

3.1.1.1. Feed Forward

In the feed forward step, the final output of a neural network is created. Let's try to find the final output of our neural network.

In our neural network, we will first find the value of zh1, which can be calculated as follows:

```
zh1 = x1w1 + x2w2 + b   ---------- (1)
```

Using zh1, we can find the value of ah1, which is:

```
ah1 = sigmoid(zh1)   ---------- (2)
```

In the same way, you find the values of ah2, ah3, and ah4.

To find the value of zo, you can use the following formula:

```
zo = ah1w9 + ah2w10 + ah3w11 + ah4w12        --------- (3)
```

Finally, to find the output of the neural network ao, use the following formula:

```
ao = sigmoid(zo)    ----------  (4)
```

3.1.1.2. Backpropagation

The purpose of backpropagation is to minimize the overall loss by finding the optimum values of weights. The loss function we are going to use in this section is the mean squared error which is in our case represented as:

$$J = \frac{1}{m} \sum_{i=1}^{m} (ao_i - y_i)^2$$

Here, ao is the predicted output from our neural network, and y is the actual output.

Our weights are divided into two parts. We have weights that connect input features to the hidden layer and the hidden layer to the output node. We call the weights that connect the input to the hidden layer collectively as wh (w1, w2, w3 ...... w8), and the weights connecting the hidden layer to the output as wo (w9, w10, w11, w12).

The backpropagation will consist of two phases. In the first phase, we will find dcost_dwo (which refers to the derivative of the total cost with respect to wo (weights in the output layer)). By chain rule, dcost_dwo can be represented as product of dcost_dao * dao_dzo * dzo_dwo. (d here refers to derivative.) Mathematically:

```
dcost_dwo = dcost_dao * dao_dzo * dzo_dwo  ------ (5)
        dcost_dao = 1/m (ao - y)   ------- (6)
dao_dzo = sigmoid(zo) * (1 - sigmoid(zo))  ------- (7)
          dzo_dwo = ah.T ------ 8
```

In the same way, you find the derivative of cost with respect to bias in the output layer, i.e., dcost_dbo, which is given as:

```
dcost_dbo = dcost_dao * dao_dzo
```

Putting 6, 7, and 8 in equation 5, we can get the derivative of cost with respect to the output weights.

The next step is to find the derivative of cost with respect to hidden layer weights, wh, and bias bh. Let's first find the derivative of cost with respect to hidden layer weights:

```
dcost_dwh  =   dcost_dah  * dah_dzh * dzh_dwh  ..... (9)
dcost_dah =  dcost_dao * dao_dzo   * dzo_dah ....... (10)
```

The values of dcost_dao and dao_dzo can be calculated from equations 6 and 7, respectively. The value of dzo_dah is given as:

```
dzo_dah = wo.T  ...... (11)
```

Putting the values of equations 6, 7, and 11 in equation 11, you can get the value of equation 10.

Next, let's find the value of dah_dzh:

```
dah_dzh = sigmoid(zh)*(1-sigmoid(zh) ..... (12)
                    and,
          dzh_dwh = X.T   (13)
```

Using equation 10, 12, and 13 in equation 9, you can find the value of dcost_dwh.

Finally, you can update the weights of the output and hidden layers as:

```
wo = wo - (lr *dcost_dwo)
wh = wh - (lr * dcost_dwh)
```

In the above equations, *wo* refers to all the weights in the output layer, whereas *wh* refers to the weights in the hidden layers.

3.1.1.3. Implementation in Python

In this section, you will implement the neural network that we saw earlier from scratch in Python.

Let's define a function that defines parameters:

Script 4:

```
1.  def define_parameters(weights):
2.      weight_list = []
3.      bias_list = []
4.      for i in range(len(weights) - 1):
5.
6.          w = np.random.randn(weights[i], weights[i+1])
7.          b = np.random.randn()
8.
9.          weight_list.append(w)
10.         bias_list.append(b)
11.
12.     return weight_list, bias_list
```

Since now, we have multiple sets of weights, the defined parameters function will return the list of weights connecting the input and hidden layer and the hidden and output layer.

Next, we define the sigmoid function and its derivative:

Script 5:

```
1.  def sigmoid(x):
2.      return 1/(1+np.exp(-x))
```

Script 6:

```
1. def sigmoid_der(x):
2.     return sigmoid(x)*(1-sigmoid(x))
```

The feed forward part of the algorithm is implemented by the **prediction()** method as shown below:

Script 7:

```
1. def predictions(w, b, X):
2.     zh = np.dot(X,w[0]) + b[0]
3.     ah = sigmoid(zh)
4.
5.     zo = np.dot(ah, w[1]) + b[1]
6.     ao = sigmoid(zo)
7.     return ao
```

The following script defines the cost function:

Script 8:

```
1. def find_cost(ao,y):
2.     m = y.shape[0]
3.     total_cost = (1/m) * np.sum(np.square(ao - y))
4.     return total_cost
```

Finally, to implement the backpropagation, we create a **derivatives()** function as follows:

Script 9:

```
1. def find_derivatives(w, b, X):
2.
3.         zh = np.dot(X,w[0]) + b[0]
4.         ah = sigmoid(zh)
5.
6.         zo = np.dot(ah, w[1]) + b[1]
7.         ao = sigmoid(zo)
8.
9.         # Back propagation phase 1
10.        m = y.shape[0]
11.        dcost_dao = (1/m)*(ao-y)
12.        dao_dzo = sigmoid_der(zo)
13.        dzo_dwo = ah.T
14.
15.        dwo = np.dot(dzo_dwo, dcost_dao * dao_dzo)
16.        dbo = np.sum(dcost_dao * dao_dzo)
17.
18.        # Back propagation phase 2
19.
20.        # dcost_wh = dcost_dah * dah_dzh * dzh_dwh
21.        # dcost_dah = dcost_dzo * dzo_dah
22.
23.        dcost_dzo = dcost_dao * dao_dzo
24.        dzo_dah = w[1].T
25.
26.        dcost_dah = np.dot(dcost_dzo,  dzo_dah)
27.
28.        dah_dzh = sigmoid_der(zh)
29.        dzh_dwh = X.T
30.        dwh = np.dot(dzh_dwh, dah_dzh * dcost_dah)
31.        dbh = np.sum(dah_dzh * dcost_dah)
32.
33.        return dwh, dbh, dwo, dbo
```

And to update weights by subtracting the gradient, we define the **update_weights()** function.

Script 10:

```
1.  def update_weights(w,b,dwh, dbh, dwo, dbo, lr):
2.       w[0] = w[0] - lr * dwh
3.       w[1] = w[1] - lr * dwo
4.
5.       b[0] = b[0] - lr * dbh
6.       b[1] = b[1] - lr * dbo
7.
8.       return w, b
```

Here is the **my_neural_network** class, which is used to train the neural network by implementing the feed forward and backward propagation steps.

Script 11:

```
1.  def my_neural_network(X, y, lr, epochs):
2.       error_list = []
3.       input_len = X.shape[1]
4.       output_len = y.shape[1]
5.       w,b = define_parameters([input_len, 4, output_len])
6.
7.       for i in range(epochs):
8.           ao = predictions(w, b, X)
9.           cost = find_cost(ao, y)
10.          error_list.append(cost)
11.          dwh, dbh, dwo, dbo = find_derivatives(w, b, X)
12.          w, b = update_weights(w, b, dwh, dbh, dwo, dbo, lr)
13.          if i % 50 == 0 :
14.              print(cost)
15.
16.      return w, b, error_list
```

Let's train our neural network now to see the error reducing:

Script 12:

```
1.  lr = 0.5
2.  epochs = 2000
3.  w, b, error_list = my_neural_network(X,y,lr,epochs)
```

Output:

```
0.1980211046202944
0.14097327813016874
0.1199356196746553
0.10996149384567079
0.1046354602995857
0.10125014770369335
0.09877988582294377
0.09681954900387213
0.09519153134310644
0.09380667924462933
0.09261322597192048
0.09157694024355723
0.09067287831113126
0.0898816633148205
0.08918762513676567
0.08857775866745798
0.0880410781190082
0.08756818639880107
0.08715097414153263
0.08678240229725143
0.08645634002244419
0.08616743928189777
0.08591103380363199
0.08568305442008338
0.0854799559120146
0.08529865252129894
0.08513646055443663
0.08499104719247362
0.08486038495701591
0.08474271141085092
0.08463649370001301
0.08454039753494193
0.08445326019470517
0.08437406713419247
0.08430193178325884
0.08423607814745766
0.0841758258488823
0.08412057727921075
0.08406980657236514
0.08402305013908634
```

In the output, you can see that the error is reducing. Let's plot the error value on a plot:

Script 13:

```
plt.plot(error_list)
```

Output:

[<matplotlib.lines.Line2D at 0x7f8e094b94e0>]

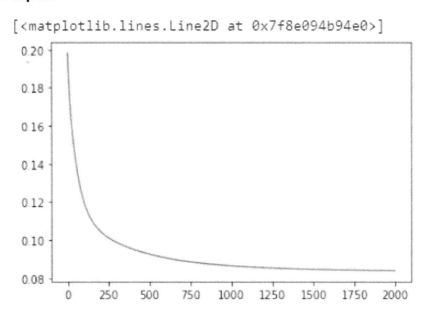

You can see that the error is decreasing with each epoch.

The process of implementing a neural network with one output from scratch in Python is very similar to logistic regression. However, in this case, we had to update two sets of weights, one in the hidden layer and one in the output layer.

3.1.2. Neural Network with Multiple Outputs

In the previous section, you did a binary classification where you predicted whether a point is red or blue. In most real-world applications, you have to classify between more than two objects. For instance, you might be given an image, and you have to guess the single digit in the image. In that case, the number of possible outputs will be 0-9 = 10. The types of problems where you have more than two possible outputs are called multiclass classification problems.

To implement multiclass classification problems, you have to make three changes in the neural network with single a output. The changes are as follows:

1. The number of nodes in the output layer should be equal to the number of possible outputs.

2. The Softmax activation function should be used in the final output layer.

3. To reduce the cost, a negative log-likelihood function should be used as the loss function.

We will not go into the details of the Softmax and negative log-likelihood functions in this chapter. Here is a very good blog to understand the Softmax function: https://bit.ly/3dXPWSY

And here is a very good blog to understand the negative log likelihood: https://bit.ly/2BYlOc7

In this section, we will develop a neural network with three possible outputs. Let's first create the dataset for that:

Execute the following script:

Script 14:

```
1.  import numpy as np
2.  import matplotlib.pyplot as plt
3.
4.  np.random.seed(42)
5.
6.  cat1 = np.random.randn(800, 2) + np.array([0, -3])
7.  cat2 = np.random.randn(800, 2) + np.array([3, 3])
8.  cat3 = np.random.randn(800, 2) + np.array([-3, 3])
9.
10. X = np.vstack([cat1, cat2, cat3])
```

```
11.
12. labels = np.array([0]*800 + [1]*800 + [2]*800)
13.
14. y = np.zeros((2400, 3))
15.
16. for i in range(2400):
17.     y[i, labels[i]] = 1
```

Let's check the shape of our dataset:

Script 15:

```
1.  print(X.shape)
2.  print(y.shape)
```

Output:

```
(2400, 2)
(2400, 3)
```

The output shows that we have 2,400 records in our dataset. The input contains two features, and the output contains three possible labels. (Each row in the output contains three columns, one column for each label.)

Next, we will plot our dataset to see the three classes:

Script 16:

```
1.  x1 = X[:,0]
2.  x2 = X[:,1]
3.
4.  plt.figure(figsize=(10,7))
5.  plt.scatter(x1, x2, c= y, cmap=plt.cm.coolwarm)
```

Output:

`<matplotlib.collections.PathCollection at 0x7f289391fe48>`

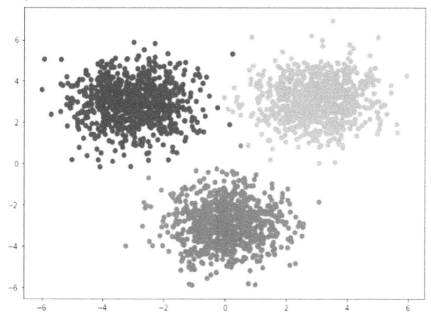

From the output, you can see that our dataset records can either be represented by a red, green, or blue dot, which means that we have three possible labels in the output. Also, these labels cannot be separated by a straight line. Hence, we will be using a neural network with multiple outputs. The architecture of the neural network will look like this:

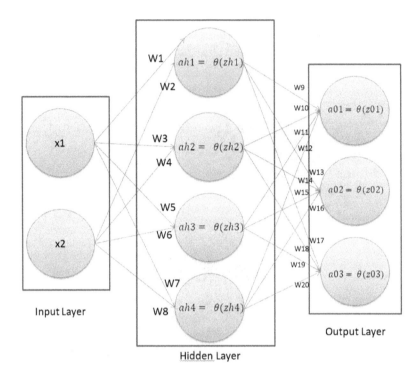

You can see that this neural network is very similar to the neural network that we saw earlier. Except, now we have three nodes in the output, and hence, a greater number of weights in the output layer. Let's see the feed forward process for the above neural network:

3.1.2.1. Feed Forward

Let's briefly review the feed forward step for a neural network with multiple steps. To calculate the value of zh1, the following equation is used:

```
zh1 = x1w1 + x2w2 + b  ---------- (14)
```

Using zh1, we can find the value of ah1, which is:

```
ah1 = sigmoid(zh1)   ---------- (15)
```

In the same way, you find the values of ah2, ah3, and ah4.

To find the value of zo, you can use the following formula:

```
zo1 = ah1w9 + ah2w10 + ah3w11 + ah4w12     --------- (16)
```

In the same way, you can calculate the values for zo2 and zo3. The output will be a vector of the form [3,1]. This vector will be passed to the Softmax function, which also returns a vector of [3,1], which will be our final output ao. Hence,

```
ao = softmax(vector [zo])   ---------- (17)
```

3.1.2.2. BackPropagation

In the backpropagation step, you have to find the derivative of the cost function with respect to the weights in different layers. Let's first find dcost_dwo:

```
dcost_dwo = dcost_dzo * dzo_dwo ------ (18)
```

The derivative of a negative log-likelihood function with respect to the values in the zo vector is:

```
dcost_dzo = ao - y -------- (19)
```

In equation 19, y is the actual output. Similarly, we can find dzo_dwo as follows:

```
dzo_dwo = ah.T ----- (20)
```

Putting 19 and 20 in 18, you can get the derivate of cost with respect to the weights in the output layer, i.e., wo.

Similarly, dcost_dbo is equal to:

```
dcost_dbo = dcost_dzo ---- (21)
```

Next, we need to find the dcost_dwh, which is given as:

```
dcost_dwh = dcost_dah *  dah_dzh * dzh_dwh ------ (22)
      dcost_dah = dcost_dzo * dzo_dah  ---- (23)
            dzo_dah = wo.T -------- (24)
```

Putting the value of equation 19 and 24 in equation 23, you can get the value of dcost_dah.

Next,

```
dah_dzh = sigmoid(zh) * (1- sigmoid(zh) ------- (25)
      dzh_dwh = ah.T ------------ (26)
```

Putting the value of 23, 25, and 26 in equation 22, you can find the value of dost_dwh.

Finally, as previously, you can update the weights of the output and hidden layers as:

```
wo = wo - (lr *dcost_dwo)
wh = wh -  (lr * dcost_dwh)
```

In the above equations, *wo* refers to all the weights in the output layer, whereas *wh* refers to the weights in the hidden layers.

3.1.2.3. Implementation in Python

Let's now see the Python implementation of a neural network with multiple outputs:

Script 17:

```
1.  import numpy as np
2.  import matplotlib.pyplot as plt
3.
4.  np.random.seed(42)
5.
6.  cat1 = np.random.randn(800, 2) + np.array([0, -3])
7.  cat2 = np.random.randn(800, 2) + np.array([3, 3])
```

```
8.  cat3 = np.random.randn(800, 2) + np.array([-3, 3])
9.
10.
11. X = np.vstack([cat1, cat2, cat3])
12.
13. labels = np.array([0]*800 + [1]*800 + [2]*800)
14.
15. y = np.zeros((2400, 3))
16.
17. for i in range(2400):
18.     y[i, labels[i]] = 1
19.
20.
21. def define_parameters(weights):
22.     weight_list = []
23.     bias_list = []
24.     for i in range(len(weights) - 1):
25.
26.         w = np.random.randn(weights[i], weights[i+1])
27.         b = np.random.randn()
28.
29.         weight_list.append(w)
30.         bias_list.append(b)
31.
32.     return weight_list, bias_list
33.
34. def softmax(X):
35.     expX = np.exp(X)
36.     return expX / expX.sum(axis=1, keepdims=True)
37.
38. def sigmoid(x):
39.     return 1/(1+np.exp(-x))
40.
41.
42. def sigmoid_der(x):
43.     return sigmoid(x)*(1-sigmoid(x))
44.
45.
46. def predictions(w, b, X):
```

```
47.     zh = np.dot(X,w[0]) + b[0]
48.     ah = sigmoid(zh)
49.
50.     zo = np.dot(ah, w[1]) + b[1]
51.     ao = softmax(zo)
52.     return ao
53.
54.
55. def find_cost(ao,y):
56.
57.     total_cost = np.sum(-y * np.log(ao))
58.     return total_cost
59.
60. def find_derivatives(w, b, X):
61.
62.     zh = np.dot(X,w[0]) + b[0]
63.     ah = sigmoid(zh)
64.
65.     zo = np.dot(ah, w[1]) + b[1]
66.     ao = softmax(zo)
67.
68.     # Back propagation phase 1
69.
70.
71.     dcost_dzo = (ao-y)
72.     dzo_dwo = ah.T
73.
74.     dwo =  np.dot(dzo_dwo,  dcost_dzo)
75.     dbo = np.sum(dcost_dzo)
76.
77.     # Back propagation phase 2
78.
79.     # dcost_wh = dcost_dah * dah_dzh * dzh_dwh
80.     # dcost_dah = dcost_dzo * dzo_dah
81.
82.
83.     dzo_dah = w[1].T
84.
85.     dcost_dah = np.dot(dcost_dzo,  dzo_dah)
```

```
86.
87.        dah_dzh = sigmoid_der(zh)
88.        dzh_dwh = X.T
89.        dwh = np.dot(dzh_dwh, dah_dzh * dcost_dah)
90.        dbh = np.sum(dah_dzh * dcost_dah)
91.
92.        return dwh, dbh, dwo, dbo
93.
94. def update_weights(w,b,dwh, dbh, dwo, dbo, lr):
95.        w[0] = w[0] - lr * dwh
96.        w[1] = w[1] - lr * dwo
97.
98.        b[0] = b[0] - lr * dbh
99.        b[1] = b[1] - lr * dbo
100.
101.       return w, b
102.
103.    def my_multiout_neural_network(X, y, lr, epochs):
104.       error_list = []
105.       input_len = X.shape[1]
106.       output_len = y.shape[1]
107.       w,b = define_parameters([input_len, 4, output_len])
108.
109.       for i in range(epochs):
110.            ao = predictions(w, b, X)
111.            cost = find_cost(ao, y)
112.            error_list.append(cost)
113.            dwh, dbh, dwo, dbo = find_derivatives (w, b, X)
114.            w, b = update_weights(w, b, dwh, dbh, dwo, dbo,
    lr)
115.            if i % 50 == 0 :
116.                print(cost)
117.
118.       return w, b, error_list
119.
120.
121.    lr = 0.0005
122.    epochs = 1000
123.    w, b, error_list = my_multiout_neural_
    network(X,y,lr,epochs)
```

Output:

```
4921.784443712775
115.05275654791413
60.7093977747567
43.422649664931626
34.88864651152795
29.785198170132094
26.38081266811703
23.942717399078127
22.107134982438154
20.67281284937415
19.519299319106253
18.570055076513714
17.774096074967886
17.09614091195548
16.51099321192574
16.000176100360964
15.549830828069574
15.149357906344129
14.790511529599819
14.466780088357714
```

The output shows that the error is decreasing. Let's plot the error against the epochs:

Script 18:

```
plt.plot(error_list)
```

Output:

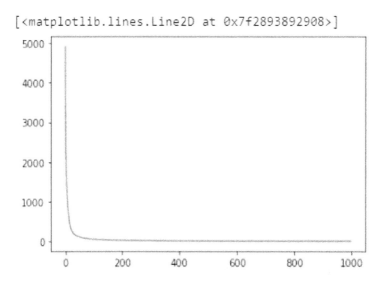

```
[<matplotlib.lines.Line2D at 0x7f2893892908>]
```

You can clearly see the error decreasing quickly initially and then very slowly.

3.1.3. Neural Network with TensorFlow Keras

In this book, you will be using the TensorFlow Keras library to develop the NLP applications.

In this section, you will be introduced to TensorFlow Keras API, using which you will be able to create Densely Connected Neural Networks for classification and regression tasks. We will be using TensorFlow 2.0 and Keras API to implement our script in this chapter. From TensorFlow 2.0, Google has officially adopted Keras as the main API to run TensorFlow scripts.

Let's begin without much ado.

The following script upgrades the existing TensorFlow version.

Script 19:

```
pip install --upgrade tensorflow
```

To check if you are actually running TensorFlow 2.0, execute the following command.

Script 20:

```
1. import tensorflow as tf
2. print(tf.__version__)
```

You should see 2.x.x in the output, as shown below:

Output:

```
2.1.0
```

Importing the Required Libraries

The following script imports the required libraries.

Script 21:

```
1. import seaborn as sns
2. import pandas as pd
3. import numpy as np
4.
5. from tensorflow.keras.layers import Dense, Dropout,
   Activation
6. from tensorflow.keras.models import Model, Sequential
7. from tensorflow.keras.optimizers import Adam
```

Importing the Dataset

The following script imports the dataset. The dataset comes prebuilt with the **Seaborn** library; therefore, you do not have to download it.

Script 22:

```
1. iris_data = sns.load_dataset('iris')
2. iris_data.head()
```

Output:

	sepal_length	sepal_width	petal_length	petal_width	species
0	5.1	3.5	1.4	0.2	setosa
1	4.9	3.0	1.4	0.2	setosa
2	4.7	3.2	1.3	0.2	setosa
3	4.6	3.1	1.5	0.2	setosa
4	5.0	3.6	1.4	0.2	setosa

Our dataset contains different attributes of the iris plant along with the species of the plant. Using the first four attributes, we have to predict the specie of the plant. There can be three possible outputs: setosa, versicolor, virginica. Since the number of target labels is greater than 2, this problem is treated as a multiclass classification problem.

Let's divide the data into features and labels set. It is important to mention that TensorFlow neural networks work with numbers. Whenever we encounter text data, we have to convert it into numbers. Our output labels are in the form of text. We can convert the output into one-hot encoded numbers using **pd.get_dummies()** method as shown below:

Script 23:

```
1. X = iris_data.drop(['species'], axis=1)
2. y = pd.get_dummies(iris_data.species, prefix='output')
3. X.head()
```

The output shows the feature set:

Output:

	sepal_length	sepal_width	petal_length	petal_width
0	5.1	3.5	1.4	0.2
1	4.9	3.0	1.4	0.2
2	4.7	3.2	1.3	0.2
3	4.6	3.1	1.5	0.2
4	5.0	3.6	1.4	0.2

The following script prints the one-hot encoded output target labels.

Script 24:

```
y.head()
```

The dimensions of the output should be R X O where R is the number of records, and O is the number of possible target variables, which in our case is 3.

Output:

	output_setosa	output_versicolor	output_virginica
0	1	0	0
1	1	0	0
2	1	0	0
3	1	0	0
4	1	0	0

The following script converts our features and labels set into numpy arrays since TensorFlow expects input data in the form of numpy arrays.

Script 25:

```
1. X = X.values
2. y = y.values
```

Dividing the Data into Training and Test Sets

The script below divides the data into training and test sets and then performs standard scaling on both the sets.

Script 26:

```
1. from sklearn.model_selection import train_test_split
2. X_train, X_test, y_train, y_test = train_test_split(X, y,
   test_size=0.20, random_state=42)
```

Script 27:

```
1. from sklearn.preprocessing import StandardScaler
2. sc = StandardScaler()
3. X_train = sc.fit_transform(X_train)
4. X_test = sc.transform(X_test)
```

Creating a Neural Network Model

As I said earlier, the neural network will be similar to the one we created for binary classification. However, in this case, the activation function in the final dense layer will be **softmax**. The number of nodes in the final dense layer will be equal to the number of target labels. And the loss function in the compile method will be **categorical_crossentropy**. Execute the following script to define the method that creates our neural network.

Script 28:

```
1.  def create_model_multiple_outs(learning_rate, dropout_
    rate):
2.
3.      model = Sequential()
4.      model.add(Dense(12, input_dim=X_train.shape[1],
    activation='relu'))
5.      model.add(Dropout(dropout_rate))
6.      model.add(Dense(6,  activation='relu'))
7.      model.add(Dropout(dropout_rate))
8.      model.add(Dense(y_train.shape[1],
    activation='softmax'))
9.
10.     adam = Adam(lr=learning_rate)
11.     model.compile(loss='categorical_crossentropy',
    optimizer=adam, metrics=['accuracy'])
12.     return model
```

The following script defines the dropout, learning rate, epochs, and batch size. You can play around with these values to see if you can get better results.

Script 29:

```
1.  dropout_rate = 0.1
2.  epochs = 50
3.  batch_size = 1
4.  learn_rate = 0.001
```

The following script creates the actual model by calling the **model_multiple_outs()** that we created in Script 25. The script also prints the structure of the neural network model, as shown by the output.

Script 30:

```
1. model = create_model_multiple_outs(learn_rate, dropout_
   rate)
2. from tensorflow.keras.utils import plot_model
3. plot_model(model, to_file='model_plot1.png', show_
   shapes=True, show_layer_names=True)
```

Output:

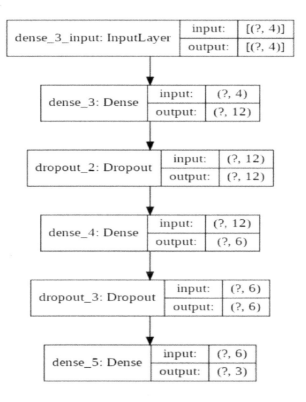

The following script trains the model by calling the **fit** method.

Script 31:

```
model_history = model.fit(X_train, y_train, batch_size=batch_
size, epochs=epochs, validation_split=0.2, verbose=1)
```

Output:

```
Epoch 45/50
96/96 [==============================] - 0s 4ms/sample - loss: 0.1804 - accuracy: 0.9375 - val_loss: 0.1126 - val_accuracy: 0.9583
Epoch 46/50
96/96 [==============================] - 0s 4ms/sample - loss: 0.1591 - accuracy: 0.9479 - val_loss: 0.0994 - val_accuracy: 0.9583
Epoch 47/50
96/96 [==============================] - 0s 4ms/sample - loss: 0.1393 - accuracy: 0.9583 - val_loss: 0.1094 - val_accuracy: 0.9583
Epoch 48/50
96/96 [==============================] - 0s 4ms/sample - loss: 0.1692 - accuracy: 0.9375 - val_loss: 0.1017 - val_accuracy: 0.9583
Epoch 49/50
96/96 [==============================] - 0s 4ms/sample - loss: 0.1428 - accuracy: 0.9375 - val_loss: 0.1001 - val_accuracy: 0.9583
Epoch 50/50
96/96 [==============================] - 0s 4ms/sample - loss: 0.1248 - accuracy: 0.9792 - val_loss: 0.1081 - val_accuracy: 0.9583
```

The output shows the result from the last five epochs. The result shows that the final accuracy of 95.83 percent is achieved on the training set.

Evaluating the Neural Network Model

The following script evaluates the model performance on the test.

Script 32:

```
1.  accuracies = model.evaluate(X_test, y_test, verbose=1)
2.
3.  print("Test Score:", accuracies[0])
4.  print("Test Accuracy:", accuracies[1])
```

Output:

```
30/30 [==============================] - 0s 3ms/sample - loss:
0.0560 - accuracy: 1.0000
Test Score: 0.0560462586581707
Test Accuracy: 1.0
```

The output shows that our model achieved 100 percent accuracy on the test set.

Let's now plot the accuracy for 50 epochs.

Script 33:

```
1.  import matplotlib.pyplot as plt
2.
3.  plt.plot(model_history.history['accuracy'], label =
    'accuracy')
4.  plt.plot(model_history.history['val_accuracy'], label =
    'val_accuracy')
5.  plt.legend(['train','test'], loc='lower left')
```

Output:

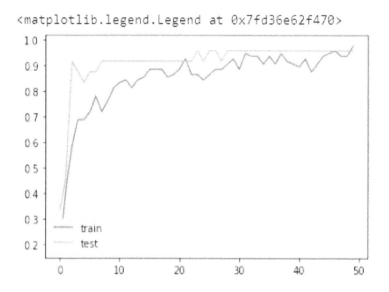

The result shows that on the training set, our model converged at around the 45th epoch. The final training and test accuracies are almost identical; therefore, we can say that our model is not overfitting.

The following script plots the loss values for the training and test sets.

Script 34:

```
1. import matplotlib.pyplot as plt
2.
3. plt.plot(model_history.history['loss'], label = 'loss')
4. plt.plot(model_history.history['val_loss'], label = 'val_
   loss')
5. plt.legend(['train','test'], loc='upper left')
```

Output:

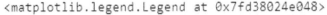

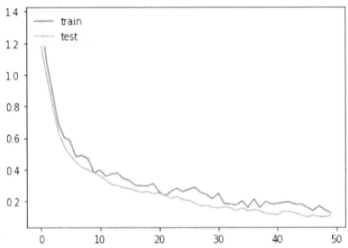

Now you know how to create densely connected neural networks for both binary and multiclass classification tasks. In the next section, you will see how to create a densely connected neural network for regression tasks.

3.2. Introduction to CNN

A convolutional neural network is a type of neural network used to classify spatial data, for instance, images, sequences, etc. In an image, each pixel is somehow related to some other pictures. Looking at a single pixel, you cannot guess the image.

Rather, you have to look at the complete picture to guess the image. A CNN does exactly that. Using a kernel or feature detects, it detects features within an image. A combination of these images then forms the complete image, which can then be classified using a densely connected neural network. One-dimensional CNN can be used to solve NLP problems.

The steps involved in a Convolutional Neural Network have been explained in the next section.

3.2.1. Image Classification with CNN

In this chapter, you will see how to perform image classification using CNN. Before we go ahead and see the steps involved in the image classification using a convolutional neural network, we first need to know how computers see images.

How Do Computers See Images?

When humans see an image, they see lines, circles, squares, and different shapes. However, a computer sees an image differently. For a computer, an image is a two—no more than a 2-D—set of pixels arranged in a certain manner. For greyscale images, the pixel value can be between 0–255, while for color images, there are three channels: red, green, and blue. Each channel can have a pixel value between 0–255. Look at the following image 5.1.

 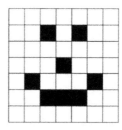 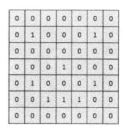

Image 5.1: How computers see images

Here, the box on the left most is what humans see. They see a smiling face. However, a computer sees it in the form of pixel values of 0s and 1s, as shown on the right-hand side. Here, 0 indicates a white pixel, whereas 1 indicates a black pixel. In the real world, 1 indicates a white pixel, while 0 indicates a black pixel.

Now, we know how a computer sees images. The next step is to explain the steps involved in the image classification using a convolutional neural network.

The following are the steps involved in image classification with CNN.

1. The Convolution Operation
2. The ReLu Operation
3. The Pooling Operation
4. Flattening and Fully Connected Layer

The Convolution Operation

The convolution operation is the first step involved in the image classification with a convolutional neural network.

In convolution operation, you have an image and a feature detector. The values of the feature detector are initialized randomly. The feature detector is moved over the image from left to right. The values in the feature detector are multiplied by the corresponding values in the image, and then all the values in the feature detector are added. The resultant value is added to the feature map.

Look at the following image, for example:

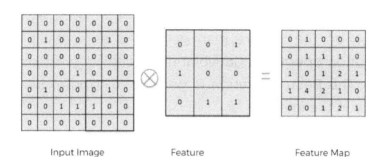

Input Image   Feature   Feature Map
                   Detector

In the above script, we have an input image of 7 x 7. The feature detector is of size 3 x 3. The feature detector is placed over the image at the top left of the input image, and then the pixel values in the feature detector are multiplied by the pixel values in the input image. The result is then added. The feature detector then moves to N steps toward the right. Here, N refers to stride. A stride is basically the number of steps that a feature detector takes from left to right, and then from top to bottom to find a new value for the feature map.

In reality, there are multiple feature detectors, as shown in the following image:

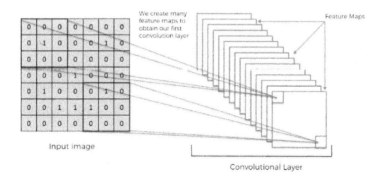

Input image   Convolutional Layer

Each feature detector is responsible for detecting a particular feature in the image.

The ReLu Operation

In ReLu operation, you simply apply the ReLu activation function on the feature map generated as a result of the convolution operation. Convolution operation gives us linear values. The ReLu operation is performed to introduce non-linearity in the image.

In the ReLu operation, all the negative values in a feature map are replaced by 0. All the positive values are left untouched.

Suppose we have the following feature map:

-4	2	1	-2
1	-1	8	0
3	-3	1	4
1	0	1	-2

When the ReLu function is applied on the feature map, the resultant feature map looks like this:

0	2	1	0
1	-0	8	0
3	0	1	4
1	0	1	0

The Pooling Operation

Pooling operation is performed in order to introduce spatial invariance in the feature map. Pooling operation is performed after convolution and ReLu operation.

Let's first understand what spatial invariance is. If you look at the following three images, you can easily identify that these images contain cheetahs.

Although the second image is disoriented and the third image is distorted, we are still able to identify that all the three images contain cheetahs based on certain features.

Pooling does exactly that. In pooling, we have a feature map and then a pooling filter, which can be of any size. Next, we move the pooling filter over the feature map and apply the pooling operation. There can be many pooling operations such as max pooling, min pooling, and average pooling. In max pooling, we choose the maximum value from the pooling filter. Pooling not only introduces spatial invariance but also reduces the size of an image.

Look at the following image. Here, in the 3rd and 4th rows and 1st and 2nd columns, we have four values 1, 0, 1, and 4. When we apply max pooling on these four pixels, the maximum value will be chosen, i.e., you can see 4 in the pooled feature map.

0	1	0	0	0
0	1	1	1	0
1	0	1	2	1
1	4	2	1	0
0	0	1	2	1

Max Pooling →

1	1	0
4	2	1
0	2	1

Feature Map

Pooled Feature Map

Flattening and Fully Connected Layer

To find more features from an image, the pooled feature maps are flattened to form a one-dimensional vector, as shown in the following figure:

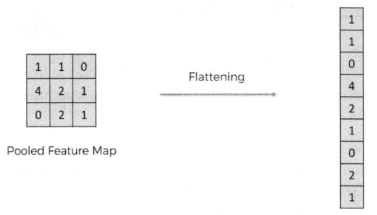

Pooled Feature Map

The one-dimensional vector is then used as input to densely or fully connected neural network layer that you will see in Chapter 4. This is shown in the following image:

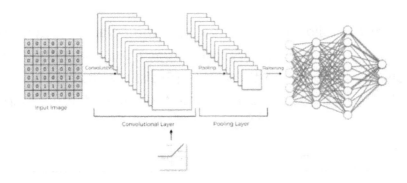

3.2.2. Implementing CNN with TensorFlow Keras

In this section, you will see how to implement CNN for image classification in TensorFlow Keras. We will create CNN that is able to classify an image of fashion items such as shirts, pants, trousers, and sandals into one of the 10 predefined categories. So, let's begin without much ado.

Execute the following script to make certain that you are running the latest version of TensorFlow.

Script 35:

```
pip install --upgrade tensorflow

import tensorflow as tf
print(tf.__version__)
```

Output:

```
2.2.0-rc1
```

The following script imports the required libraries and classes.

Script 36:

```
1. import numpy as np
2. import matplotlib.pyplot as plt
3.
4. from tensorflow.keras.layers import Input, Conv2D, Dense,
   Flatten, Dropout, MaxPool2D
5.
6. from tensorflow.keras.models import Model
```

The following script downloads the Fashion MNIST dataset that contains images of different fashion items along with their labels. The script divides the data into training images and training labels and test images and test labels.

Script 37:

```
1. mnist_data = tf.keras.datasets.fashion_mnist
2.
3. (training_images, training_labels), (test_images, test_
   labels) = mnist_data .load_data()
```

The images in our dataset are greyscale images, where each pixel value lies between 0 and 255. The following script normalizes pixel values between 0 and 1.

Script 38:

```
training_images, test_images = training_images/255.0, test_
images/255.0
```

Let's print the shape of our training data.

Script 39:

```
print(training_images.shape)
```

Output:

```
(60000, 28, 28)
```

The above output shows that our training dataset contains sixty thousand records (images). Each image is 28 pixels wide and 28 pixels high.

Let's print an image randomly from the test set:

Script 40:

```
1. plt.figure()
2. plt.imshow(test_images[9])
3. plt.colorbar()
4. plt.grid(False)
5. plt.show()
```

Output:

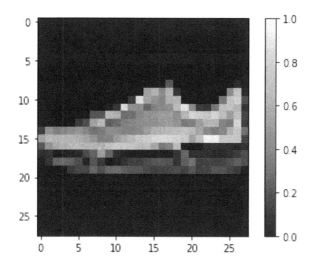

The output shows that the 9th image in our test set is the image of a sneaker.

The next step is to change the dimensions of our input images. CNN in Keras expects data to be in the format Width-Height-Channels. Our images contain width and height but no channels. Since the images are grayscale, we set the image channel to 1, as shown in the following script:

Script 41:

```
1. training_images = np.expand_dims(training_images, -1)
2. test_images = np.expand_dims(test_images, -1)
3. print(training_images.shape)
```

Output:

```
(60000, 28, 28, 1)
```

The next step is to find the number of output classes. This number will be used to define the number of neurons in the output layer.

Script 42:

```
1. output_classes = len(set(training_labels))
2. print("Number of output classes is: ", output_classes)
```

Output:

```
Number of output classes is:  10
```

As expected, the number of output classes in our dataset is 10.

Let's print the shape of a single image in the training set.

Script 43:

```
training_images[0].shape
```

Output:

```
(28, 28, 1)
```

The shape of a single image is (28, 28, 1). This shape will be used to train our convolutional neural network. The following script creates a model for our convolutional neural network.

Script 44:

```
1. input_layer = Input(shape = training_images[0].shape)
2.
3. conv1 = Conv2D(32, (3,3), strides = 2, activation= 'relu')
   (input_layer)
4.
5. maxpool1 = MaxPool2D(2, 2)(conv1)
6.
7. conv2 = Conv2D(64, (3,3), strides = 2, activation= 'relu')
   (maxpool1)
8.
9. flat1 = Flatten()(conv2)
10.
11. drop1 = Dropout(0.2)(flat1)
12.
13. dense1 = Dense(512, activation = 'relu')(drop1)
14.
```

```
15. drop2   = Dropout(0.2)(dense1)
16.
17. output_layer = Dense(output_classes, activation=
    'softmax')(drop2)
18.
19. model = Model(input_layer, output_layer)
```

The model contains one input layer, two convolutional layers, one flattening layer, one hidden dense layer, and one output layer. The number of filters in the first convolutional layer is 32, while the second convolutional layer is 64. The kernel size for both convolutional layers is 3 x 3, with a stride of 2. After the first convolutional layer, a max-pooling layer with a size 2 x 2 and stride 2 has also been defined.

It is important to mention that while defining the model layers, we use Keras Functional API. With Keras functional API, to connect the previous layer with the next layer, the name of the previous layer is passed inside the parenthesis at the end of the next layer.

The following line compiles the model.

Script 45:

```
model.compile(optimizer = 'adam', loss= 'sparse_categorical_
crossentropy', metrics =['accuracy'])
```

Finally, execute the following script to print the model architecture.

Script 46:

```
1.  from tensorflow.keras.utils import plot_model
2.  plot_model(model, to_file='model_plot1.png', show_
    shapes=True, show_layer_names=True)
```

Output:

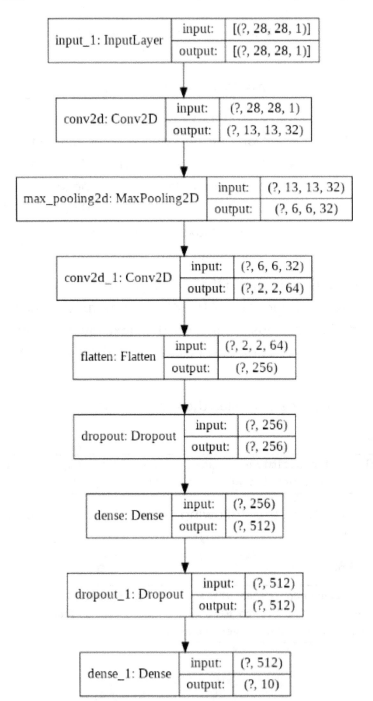

The following script trains the image classification model.

Script 47:

```
model_history = model.fit(training_images, training_labels,
epochs=20, validation_data=(test_images, test_labels),
verbose=1)
```

The results from the last five epochs are shown in the output.

Output:

```
Epoch 16/20
1875/1875 [==============================] - 5s 2ms/step - loss: 0.2318 - accuracy: 0.9107 - val_loss: 0.3217 - val_accuracy: 0.8843
Epoch 17/20
1875/1875 [==============================] - 4s 2ms/step - loss: 0.2269 - accuracy: 0.9129 - val_loss: 0.3268 - val_accuracy: 0.8870
Epoch 18/20
1875/1875 [==============================] - 4s 2ms/step - loss: 0.2224 - accuracy: 0.9147 - val_loss: 0.3379 - val_accuracy: 0.8814
Epoch 19/20
1875/1875 [==============================] - 4s 2ms/step - loss: 0.2164 - accuracy: 0.9174 - val_loss: 0.3279 - val_accuracy: 0.8846
Epoch 20/20
1875/1875 [==============================] - 4s 2ms/step - loss: 0.2112 - accuracy: 0.9192 - val_loss: 0.3277 - val_accuracy: 0.8882
```

Let's plot the training and test accuracies for our model.

Script 48:

```
1. import matplotlib.pyplot as plt
2.
3. plt.plot(model_history.history['accuracy'], label =
   'accuracy')
4. plt.plot(model_history.history['val_accuracy'], label =
   'val_accuracy')
5. plt.legend(['train','test'], loc='lower left')
```

The following output shows that training accuracy is higher, and test accuracy starts to flatten after 88 percent. We can say that our model is overfitting.

Output:

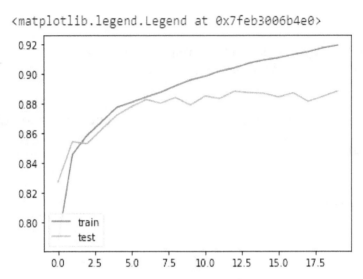

```
<matplotlib.legend.Legend at 0x7feb3006b4e0>
```

Let's make a prediction on one of the images in the test set. Let's predict the label for image 9. We know that image 9 contains a sneaker, as we saw earlier by plotting the image.

Script 49:

```
1. output = model.predict(test_images)
2. prediction = np.argmax(output[9])
3. print(prediction)
```

Output:

```
7
```

The output shows number 7. The output will always be a number since deep learning algorithms work only with numbers. The numbers correspond to the following labels.

0: T-shirt\top

1: Trousers

2: Pullover

3: Dress

4: Coat

5: Sandal

6: Shirt

7: Sneaker

8: Bag

9: Ankle boot

The above list shows that number 7 corresponds to sneakers. Hence, the prediction by our CNN is correct.

In this section, you saw an application of a convolutional neural network for image classification. CNN is also used for sequence problems such as sentence classification and stock market prediction. In part 2 of this book, you will see how a 1-dimensional convolutional neural network can be used for sentiment classification task from text reviews.

3.3. Introduction to RNN

Recurrent neural networks and its variants have proven to be some of the most useful algorithms for various natural language processing tasks.

This section explains what a recurrent neural network (RNN) is, what is the problem with RNN, and how a long short-term memory network (LSTM) can be used to solve the problems with RNN.

3.3.1. What Is an RNN?

A recurrent neural network is a type of neural network that is used to process data that is sequential in nature. Sequential data is a type of data where the value of data at timestep T depends upon the values of data at timesteps less than T, for instance, sound waves, text sentences, stock market prices, etc. In the stock market price prediction problem, the value of the opening price of a stock at a given data depends upon the opening stock price of the previous days.

The difference between the architecture of a recurrent neural network and a simple neural network is presented in the following figure:

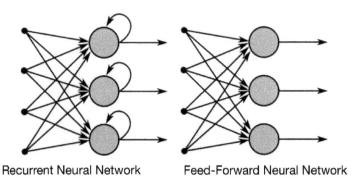

Recurrent Neural Network   Feed-Forward Neural Network

In recurrent neural network, at each timestep, the previous output of the neuron is also multiplied by the current input via a weight vector. You can see from the above figure that the output from a neuron is looped back into for the next timestep. The following figure makes this concept further clear:

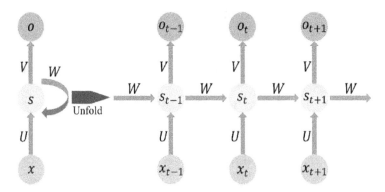

Here, we have a single neuron with one input and one output. On the right side, the process followed by a recurrent neural network is unfolded. You can see that at timestep t, the input is multiplied by weight vector U, while the previous output at time t−1, i.e., St−1 is multiplied by the weight vector W, the sum of the input vector XU + SW becomes the output at time T. This is how a recurrent neural network captures the sequential information.

3.3.2. Problems with RNN

A problem with the recurrent neural network is that while it can capture a shorter sequence, it tends to forget longer sequences.

For instance, it is easier to predict the missing word in the following sentence because the Keyword "Birds" is present in the same sentence.

"Birds fly in the ___."

RNN can easily guess that the missing word is "Clouds" here.

However, RNN cannot remember longer sequences such as the one …

> *"Mike grew up in France. He likes to each cheese, he plays piano…………………………………………………………………………*
>
> *……………………………………………………………………………………………………,*
>
> *and he speaks _____ fluently."*

Here, the RNN can only guess that the missing word is "French" if it remembers the first sentence, i.e., "Mike grew up in France."

The recurrent neural networks consist of multiple recurrent layers, which results in a diminishing gradient problem. The diminishing gradient problem is that during the backpropagation of the recurrent layer, the gradient of the earlier layer becomes infinitesimally small, which virtually makes neural network initial layers stop from learning anything.

To solve this problem, a special type of recurrent neural network, i.e., Long Short-Term Memory (LSTM) has been developed.

3.4. LSTM for improving Retention

3.4.1. What Is an LSTM?

LSTM is a type of RNN, which is capable of remembering longer sequences and hence is one of the most commonly used RNN for sequence tasks.

In LSTM, instead of a single unit in the recurrent cell, there are four interacting units, i.e., a forget gate, an input gate, an update gate, and an output gate. The overall architecture of an LSTM cell is shown in the following figure:

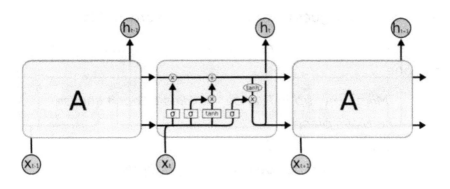

LSTM: Single Input - Single Output

Let's briefly discuss all the components of an LSTM:

Cell State

The cell state in LSTM is responsible for remembering a long sequence. The following figure describes the cell state:

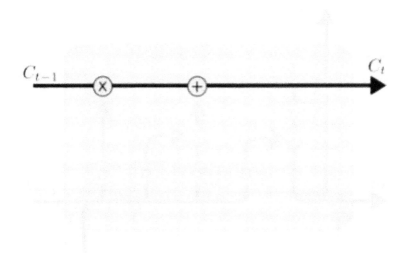

The cell state contains data from all the previous cells in the sequence. The LSTM is capable of adding or removing information to a cell state. In other words, the LSTM tells the cell state which part of previous information to remember and which information to forget.

Forget Gate

The forget gate basically tells the cell state which information to retain from the information in the previous step and which information to forget. The working and calculation formula for the forget gate is as follows:

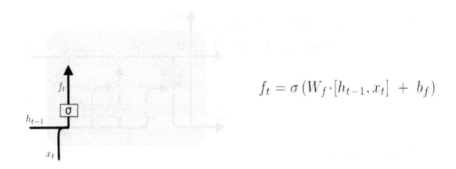

$$f_t = \sigma\left(W_f \cdot [h_{t-1}, x_t] + b_f\right)$$

Input Gate

The forget gate is used to decide which information to remember or forget. The input gate is responsible for updating or adding any new information in the cell state. The input gate has two parts: an input layer, which decides which part of the cell state is to be updated, and a tanh layer, which actually creates a vector of new values that are added or replaced in the cell state. The working of the input gate is explained in the following figure:

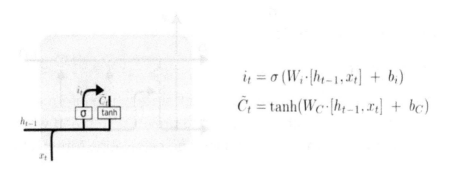

$$i_t = \sigma\left(W_i \cdot [h_{t-1}, x_t] + b_i\right)$$
$$\tilde{C}_t = \tanh(W_C \cdot [h_{t-1}, x_t] + b_C)$$

Update Gate

The forget gate tells us what to forget, and the input gate tells us what to add to the cell state. The next step is to actually perform these two operations. The update gate is basically used to perform these two operations. The functioning and the equations for the update gate are as follows:

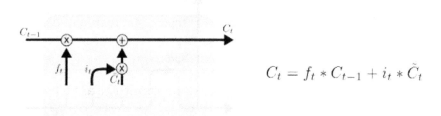

$$C_t = f_t * C_{t-1} + i_t * \tilde{C}_t$$

Output Gate

Finally, you have the output gate which outputs hidden state and the output just like a common recurrent neural network. The additional output from an LSTM node is cell state, which runs between all the nodes in a sequence. The equations and the functioning of the output gate are depicted by the following figure:

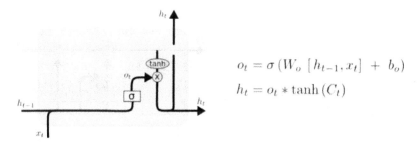

$$o_t = \sigma \left(W_o \left[h_{t-1}, x_t \right] + b_o \right)$$
$$h_t = o_t * \tanh \left(C_t \right)$$

In the following sections, you will see how to implement LSTM for sequence classification.

3.4.2. Implementing LSTM with Keras

In this section, you will implement a very simple LSTM with a sequence of input features and a single output feature.

The following script imports the required libraries:

Script 50:

```
import numpy as np
import matplotlib.pyplot as plt
from tensorflow.keras.layers import Input, Activation, Dense,
    Flatten, Dropout,  Flatten, LSTM
from tensorflow.keras.models import Model
```

Let's first create our feature set. Our input dataset will have two features. The first feature consists of multiples of 4 from 4 to 160, whereas the second feature consists of multiples of 5 from 5 to 200.

Script 51:

```
1. X1 = np.array([x+4 for x in range(0, 160, 4)])
2. print(X1)
3.
4. X2 = np.array([x+5 for x in range(0, 200, 5)])
5. print(X2)
```

Output:

```
[   4    8   12   16   20   24   28   32   36   40   44   48   52   56   60
  64   68   72   76   80   84   88   92   96  100  104  108  112  116  120  124
 128  132  136  140  144  148  152  156  160]
[   5   10   15   20   25   30   35   40   45   50   55   60   65   70   75
  80   85   90   95  100  105  110  115  120  125  130  135  140  145  150  155
 160  165  170  175  180  185  190  195  200]
```

Next, we stack our two features together.

Script 52:

```
1. X = np.column_stack((X1, X2))
2. print(X)
```

Output:

```
[[  4   5]
 [  8  10]
 [ 12  15]
 [ 16  20]
 [ 20  25]
 [ 24  30]
 [ 28  35]
 [ 32  40]
 [ 36  45]
 [ 40  50]
 [ 44  55]
 [ 48  60]
 [ 52  65]
 [ 56  70]
 [ 60  75]
 [ 64  80]
 [ 68  85]
 [ 72  90]
 [ 76  95]
 [ 80 100]
 [ 84 105]
 [ 88 110]
 [ 92 115]
 [ 96 120]
 [100 125]
 [104 130]
 [108 135]
 [112 140]
 [116 145]
 [120 150]
 [124 155]
 [128 160]
 [132 165]
 [136 170]
 [140 175]
 [144 180]
 [148 185]
```

```
[152 190]
[156 195]
[160 200]]
```

Finally, we reshape our feature set so that each record has two timesteps, and one timestep consists of two features.

Script 53:

```
1.  X = np.array(X).reshape(20, 2, 2)
2.  print(X)
```

Output:

```
[[[  4    5]
  [  8   10]]

 [[ 12   15]
  [ 16   20]]

 [[ 20   25]
  [ 24   30]]

 [[ 28   35]
  [ 32   40]]

 [[ 36   45]
  [ 40   50]]

 [[ 44   55]
  [ 48   60]]

 [[ 52   65]
  [ 56   70]]

 [[ 60   75]
  [ 64   80]]

 [[ 68   85]
  [ 72   90]]
```

```
[[ 76  95]
 [ 80 100]]

[[ 84 105]
 [ 88 110]]

[[ 92 115]
 [ 96 120]]

[[100 125]
 [104 130]]

[[108 135]
 [112 140]]

[[116 145]
 [120 150]]

[[124 155]
 [128 160]]

[[132 165]
 [136 170]]

[[140 175]
 [144 180]]

[[148 185]
 [152 190]]

[[156 195]
 [160 200]]]
```

The output is simply the sum of two features in the two timesteps for each input record.

Script 54:

```
1. y = [sum (y) for y in [sum(x) for x in X]]
2. y = np.array(y)
3. print(y)
```

Output:

```
[ 27  63  99 135 171 207 243 279 315 351 387 423 459 495 531
567 603 639 675 711]
```

Next, we will create our neural network. This neural network is very similar to the one we created earlier in the previous section. However, the shape of the input layer is different here since we have two input steps instead of one and two features per input step.

Script 55:

```
1. input_layer = Input(shape = (2,2))
2. lstm1 = LSTM(100, activation='relu', return_
   sequences=True)(input_layer)
3. lstm2 = LSTM(50, activation='relu', return_sequences=True)
   (lstm1)
4. lstm3 = LSTM(25, activation='relu') (lstm2)
5. dense1 = Dense(10, activation='relu')(lstm3)
6. output_layer = Dense(1)(dense1)
7. model = Model(input_layer, output_layer)
8. model.compile(optimizer='adam', loss='mse')
```

The following script displays the architecture of our model.

Script 56:

```
1. from tensorflow.keras.utils import plot_model
2. plot_model(model, to_file='model_plot1.png', show_
   shapes=True, show_layer_names=True)
```

Output:

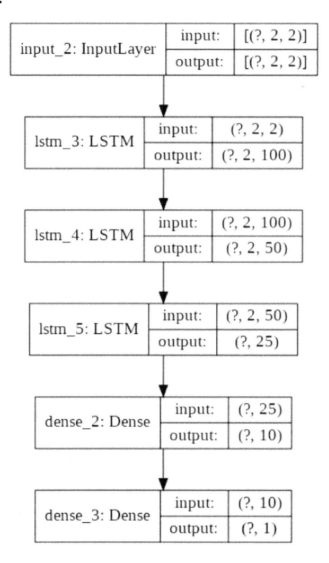

Finally, execute the following script to train the model.

Script 57:

```
model_history = model.fit(X, y, epochs=1000, verbose=1)
```

The loss value achieved at the end of the 1000th epoch has been printed below:

Output:

```
Epoch 996/1000
1/1 [==========================] - 0s 1ms/step - loss: 0.0318
Epoch 997/1000
1/1 [==========================] - 0s 811us/step - loss: 0.0316
Epoch 998/1000
1/1 [==========================] - 0s 892us/step - loss: 0.0315
Epoch 999/1000
1/1 [==========================] - 0s 782us/step - loss: 0.0314
Epoch 1000/1000
1/1 [==========================] - 0s 766us/step - loss: 0.0313
```

Note: Since initial weights of a neural network are randomly initialized in above scripts, you might get a slightly different result.

We can also plot the values for the loss with respect to epochs using the following script.

Script 58:

```
1. import matplotlib.pyplot as plt
2.
3. plt.plot(model_history.history['loss'], label = 'loss')
4. plt.legend(['train'], loc='top right')
```

Output:

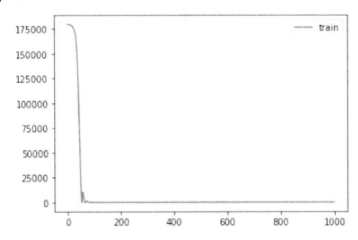

You can see that the minimum error value is achieved around the 60th epoch.

Let's test our code. We have a test record with two timesteps and two features per timestep. The actual output value is 859.

Script 59:

```
1. X_test = np.array([[200, 225], ## 859
2.                    [204,230]])
3. X_test = X_test.reshape((1, 2, 2))
4. y_pred = model.predict(X_test, verbose=0)
5. print(y_pred)
```

Our model predicts 860.60, which is extremely close to 859, which shows that our model is working perfectly fine.

Output:

```
[[860.6011]]
```

3.5. Seq2Seq Models with LSTM

An LSTM can be used to develop a neural network where the input consists of multiple sizes, and the output also consists of multiple sizes. Such a type of LSTM is called many to many LSTM.

Many to many sequence problems are further divided into two types: problems where the size of inputs and output sequences are fixed, and the problems where the input and output both have varying sizes for every record. The second type of problem is also known as sequence two sequence (seq2seq) model. In the following figure, the image on the left corresponds to the seq2seq model, while the image on the right shows a simple many to many models with a fixed input and output sizes.

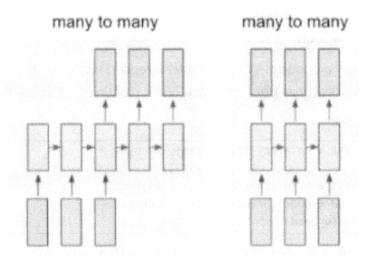

Here is an example of a sequence 2 sequence model. This seq2seq model translates English sentences into French. A seq2seq model consists of an encoder and a decoder.

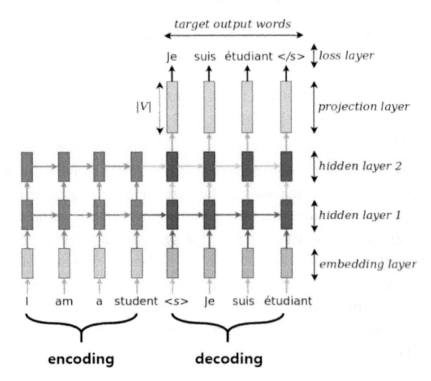

The input to the encoder is a text sentence of varying length, and the output is the LSTM output of the text. The input to the decoder is the output from the encoder LSTM, plus the actual output sequence offset by one step. The output is the corresponding actual output sequence.

3.5.1. Encoder

In the following figure, the blue rectangles correspond to the encoder layers. The encoder is basically an LSTM that accepts a text sentence as an input and output numeric representation of text. For instance, the input "I am a student" is used as input, and the corresponding output is any number.

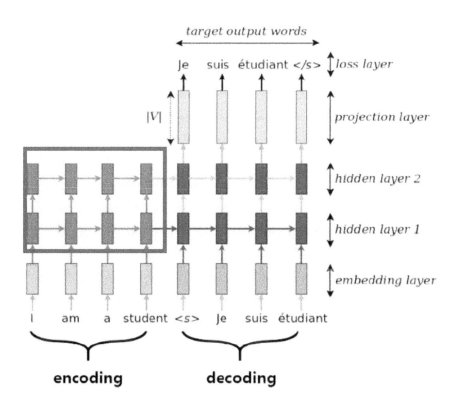

3.5.2. Decoder

Decoder is another LSTM. The input to the decoder is the hidden and cell states from the encoder LSTMs plus the actual output sequence offset by one. For instance, you can see that in the first decoder layer (shown in pink), the input to the first node is an empty string, i.e., <s> and the hidden state and cell state from the encoder. The output for the first node is the word "je," which stands for "I" in French. The input to the second node in the decoder is the word "Je" and the hidden and cell state from the previous cell in the decoder. This is shown in the following figure:

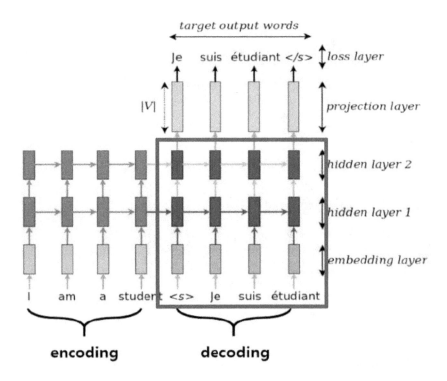

The output from the decoder is the actual output sequence, i.e., "Je suis etudinant </s>." The placeholder "</s>" tells the decoder that this is the end of the output sequence.

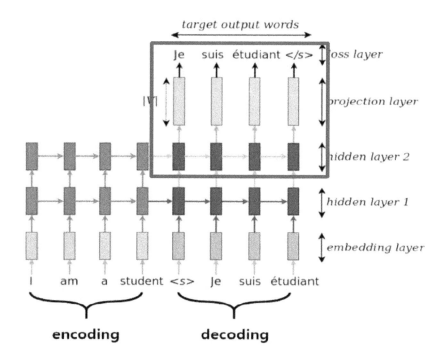

The output is actually consisting of a series of one-hot encoded vectors, as shown below. The difference between the predicted and actual output values is used to calculate the error, which is then propagated back to the decoder and encoder LSTM. The error can then be reduced via the gradient descent algorithm.

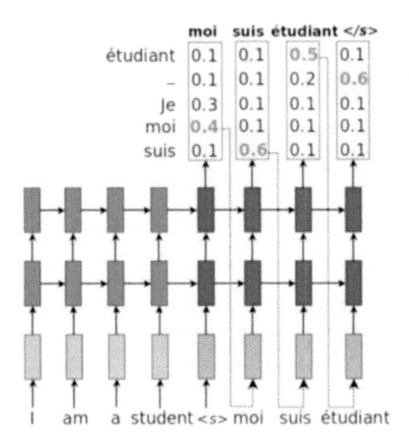

	moi	suis	étudiant	</s>
étudiant	0.1	0.1	0.5	0.1
–	0.1	0.1	0.2	0.6
Je	0.3	0.1	0.1	0.1
moi	0.4	0.1	0.1	0.1
suis	0.1	0.6	0.1	0.1

I   am   a student <s> moi   suis étudiant

3.5.3. Making Predictions

To make a prediction, the whole input sentence is passed as input to the encoder. The final hidden and cell states from the encoder are passed to the first decoder layer. The input to the decoder is the empty tag "<s>". Using the hidden and cell states from the encoder and the input "<s>" the first decoder output is the first translated word, which is "Je" in the following figure. In the second step, the output from the first step, i.e., "Je," and the hidden and cell states from the previous node are used to predict the next word, which is "suis." The process continues until the decoder predicts "</s>" tag, which corresponds to the end of the output. It is important to mention that tags don't have to be "<s>" or "</s>." Rather, tags can be any special character, as well.

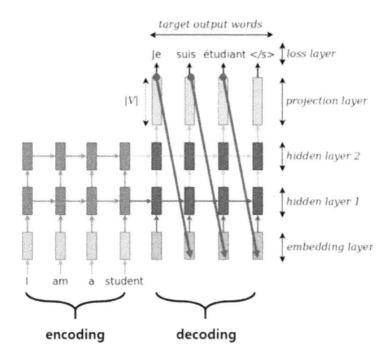

In this chapter, you saw RNN, LSTM, and CNN. You also studied how to solve sequence problems using these deep learning algorithms. In chapters 9, 10, and 11, you will see the practical implementations of these neural networks.

Further Readings – Deep Learning for NLP

To learn more about RNN, LSTM, CNN, and Seq2Seq, check these links:

https://bit.ly/3fxh5wr (For RNN and LSTM)
https://bit.ly/2YNairE (For CNN)
https://bit.ly/2Y8L9Zn (For Seq2Seq)

Hands-on Time – Exercise

Now, it is your turn. Follow the instructions in **the exercises below** to check your understanding of the RNN, LSTM, and CNN. The answers to these questions are given at the end of the book.

Exercise 3.1.

Question 1:

In a neural network with three input features, one hidden layer of five nodes, and an output layer of three possible values, what will be the dimensions of weight that connects the input to the hidden layer? Remember, the dimensions of the input data are (m,3), where m is the number of records.

A. [5,3]

B. [3,5]

C. [4,5]

D. [5,4]

Question 2:

The pooling layer is used to pick correct features even if:

A. Image is inverted

B. Image is distorted

C. Image is compressed

D. All of the above

Question 3:

The shape of the feature set passed to the LSTM's input layer should be:

A. Number of Records, Features, Timesteps

B. Timesteps, Features, Number of Records

C. Features, Timesteps, Number of Records

D. Number of Records, Timesteps, Features

Exercise 3.2.

Using the CFAR 10 image dataset, perform image classification to recognize. Here is the dataset:

```
cifar_dataset = tf.keras.datasets.cifar10
```

Text Cleaning and Manipulation

Before you can use text to train statistical algorithms, you will need to perform several preprocessing tasks such as text cleaning, parts of speech tagging, stop word removal, stemming, lemmatization, etc.

In this chapter, you will see how to perform text cleaning and manipulation with Python. You will often need to perform custom text cleaning and manipulation before you can use the text to perform various tasks. For instance, you might want to remove all the special characters before you perform text classification. Or you may want to retain only numbers in your text.

In Python, the text is treated as a string type. Therefore, string manipulation libraries such as Regex can be used for text cleaning and manipulation. In addition, you can use default string functions to clean and manipulate strings. In this chapter, you will see both approaches.

4.1. Introduction to Regular Expressions

Regular Expressions, also known as Regex, is a sequence of characters used to match a pattern of strings inside some text. Once a pattern is matched, you can apply different functions on that pattern. For instance, you can substitute values on a string, and depending upon the regex pattern, you can add or remove values from text, you can search values inside a text, etc. In this section, you will learn about some of the most useful regex expressions in Python.

The following script imports the regex module into your Python application.

Script 1:

```
import re
```

4.2. Searching and Matching Patterns in Text

To search a pattern inside a string, you can either use search or match functions. Let's first see how to use the match function.

Let's declare a variable sentence with some text:

Script 2:

```
sentence = "France won the FIFA World Cup 2018"
```

Next, we will define a regex pattern and will check which part of the text in the sentence variable matches the regex pattern.

Script 3:

```
1. output = re.match(r".*", sentence)
2. print(output)
```

In the above script, we define a regex pattern ".*" which matches any string. If you print the output, you should see the following text. The text contains the matched string, the matched character index, i.e., span, and the matched object.

Output:

```
<re.Match object; span=(0, 34), match='France won the FIFA
World Cup 2018'>
```

To print the matched string, you can use the group(0) attribute of the returned regex object, as shown below:

Script 4:

```
print(output.group(0))
```

Output:

```
France won the FIFA World Cup 2018
```

From the output, you can see that the whole string has been matched. This is because the ".*" expression matches any string even if a string is empty, as shown below:

Script 5:

```
1.  sentence = ""
2.  output = re.match(r".*", sentence)
3.  print(output)
```

The output again returns a match, i.e., the empty string.

Output:

```
<re.Match object; span=(0, 0), match=''>
```

If you want to match all strings that are at least of length one or contain one character, you can use the ".+" regex expression as shown below:

Script 6:

```
1. sentence = ""
2. output = re.match(r".+", sentence)
3. print(output)
```

Now, the empty string stored in the sentence variable has not been matched.

Output:

```
None
```

Next, let's match all the alphabets in a string. The pattern used is "[a-zA-z]," which means that match lower case alphabets from a to z, match upper case alphabets from A to Z, and match single space as well. Here is the script.

Script 7:

```
1. sentence = "France won the FIFA World Cup 2018"
2. output = re.match(r"[a-zA-z ]+", sentence)
3. print(output.group())
```

The following is the output.

Output:

```
France won the FIFA World
```

The match function only matches the string from the start. If a match is not found at the beginning of a string, the match function returns none. For instance, the match function in the following example will return none since the string starts with a digit, whereas the regex pattern in the match function searches for alphabets.

Script 8:

```
1. sentence = "2018 was the year when France won the FIFA
   World Cup"
2. output = re.match(r"[a-zA-z ]+", sentence)
3. print(output)
```

Output:

```
None
```

To solve the problem explained in the above script, the search function is used. The search function looks for the Regex pattern not only at the beginning of the string but also anywhere in the string. The following regex pattern will skip the integer at the beginning of the string and will return the remaining text.

Script 9:

```
1. sentence = "2018 was the year when France won the FIFA
   World Cup"
2. output = re.search(r"[a-zA-z ]+", sentence)
3. print(output.group(0))
```

Output:

```
was the year when France won the FIFA World Cup
```

4.3. Substituting Text in Strings

To substitute text in a string, the sub()-function from the Regex module is used. For instance, the following script substitutes 2018 by 1998 in the sentence string.

Script 10:

```
1. sentence = "France won the FIFA World Cup 2018"
2. output = re.sub(r"2018", "1998", sentence)
3. print(output)
```

Output:

```
France won the FIFA World Cup 1998
```

Similarly, the following script finds all the small case alphabets from a to f and replaces them with an asterisk.

Script 11:

```
1. sentence = "France won the FIFA World Cup 2018"
2. output = re.sub(r"[a-f]", "*", sentence)
3. print(output)
```

Output:

```
Fr*n** won th* FIFA Worl* Cup 2018
```

4.4. Removing Digits and Alphabets from a String

The "sub()"-function can also be used to remove digits, alphabets, or special characters from a string. All you have to do is specify a regex pattern that finds the alphabets or digits that you want to remove and replace them with an empty string without space.

The following script finds all digits and replaces them with an empty string. In the output, you will see that digits are removed. **Note**: The regex pattern to find digits is \d.

Script 12:

```
1. sentence = "France won the FIFA World Cup 2018"
2. output = re.sub(r"\d", "", sentence)
3. print(output)
```

Output:

```
France won the FIFA World
```

Sometimes, removing an alphabet results in a single alphabet with no meaning. For instance, in the following example, there is an "a" at the end of the string. To remove such alphabets, the regex expression "\s+[a-zA-Z]\+s" is used. Here is an example.

Script 13:

```
1.  sentence = "France won the FIFA World Cup 2018 a "
2.  result = re.sub(r"\s+[a-zA-Z]\s+", " ", sentence)
3.  print(result)
```

Output:

```
France won the FIFA World Cup 2018
```

The following script is used to remove all the alphabets. Here, the regex expression specified is [a-z]. The attribute "flags = re.I" is used to remove case sensitivity. Hence both upper- and lower-case alphabets are replaced by empty spaces.

Script 14:

```
1.  sentence = "France won the FIFA World Cup 2018"
2.  output = re.sub(r"[a-z]", "", sentence, flags =re.I)
3.  print(output)
```

Removing alphabets resulted in multiple empty spaces, as shown below:

Output:

```
2018
```

Let's see how to remove multiple empty spaces.

4.5. Removing Empty Spaces from Strings

To remove empty spaces from the text, you need to substitute empty spaces with an empty string having no space, as shown below.

Script 15:

```
1. sentence = "2018"
2. output = re.sub(r"\s+", "", sentence, flags =re.I)
3. print(output)
```

Output:

```
2018
```

4.6. Removing Special Characters from Strings

Special characters are symbols other than alphabets and digits, for example, @, /, *, &, etc. You often need to remove all the special characters from the text before using the text to perform any NLP task. The pattern to find everything except special characters is \w. You can select special characters by inverting \w. The ""^"" operator is used to invert a regex expression. Therefore, the regex expression "[\^w]" would mean select special characters only. Next, you can replace special characters with a space.

Script 16:

```
1. sentence = "Fr@nce won // the + - & * FIFA World Cup 2018"
2. output = re.sub(r"[^\w ]", "", sentence, flags =re.I)
3. print(output)
```

Output:

```
Frnce won   the     FIFA World Cup 2018
```

Similarly, the following regex expression matches everything except small and large case alphabets and digits from 1-9, which leaves special characters behind. The special characters are then replaced by an empty string.

Script 17:

```
1.  sentence = "Fr@nce won // the + - & * FIFA World Cup 2018"
2.  output = re.sub(r"[^a-zA-z0-9 ]", "", sentence, flags
    =re.I)
3.  print(output
```

Output:

```
Frnce won   the      FIFA World Cup 2018
```

4.7. Miscellaneous String Functions

Apart from regex, Python contains some default functions for string manipulation. In this chapter, you will see some of these functions.

4.7.1. Finding String Length

String length refers to the number of characters in a string. The **len()** function is used to find the length of a string.

Script 18:

```
1.  sentence = "France won the FIFA World Cup 2018"
2.  print(len(sentence))
```

Output:

```
34
```

4.7.2. Joining Strings

The easiest way to join two or more strings is via the addition operator, as shown in the following example.

Script 19:

```
1.  sentence1 = "France won the"
2.  sentence2 = "FIFA World Cup 2018"
3.  output = sentence1 + sentence2
4.  print(output)
```

Output:

```
France won the FIFA World Cup 2018
```

4.7.3. Finding Start and End of a String

To find if a string starts with a specific substring, you can use the **startswith()** function.

Script 20:

```
1.  sentence = "France won the FIFA World Cup 2018"
2.  print(sentence.startswith("France"))
```

Output:

```
True
```

Similarly, to find if a string ends with a specific substring, you can use the **endswith()** function.

Script 21:

```
1.  sentence = "France won the FIFA World Cup 2018"
2.  print(sentence.endswith("France"))
```

Output:

```
False
```

4.7.4. Changing String Case

You can convert a string into lower and uppercase using **lower()** and **upper()** functions, respectively.

The following script converts a string into lower case.

Script 22:

```
1. sentence = "France won the FIFA World Cup 2018"
2. print(sentence.lower())
```

Output:

```
france won the fifa world cup 2018
```

Similarly, the script below converts a string into upper case.

Script 23:

```
1. sentence = "France won the FIFA World Cup 2018"
2. print(sentence.upper())
```

Output:

```
FRANCE WON THE FIFA WORLD CUP 2018
```

4.7.5. Finding a Substring in Strings

To find if a string exists in another string, you can use the "in" operator, as shown in the following two examples. The in operator returns True if a substring is found inside another string and returns false if a substring is not present in another string.

Here is an example where a substring is found inside another string.

Script 24:

```
1. sentence = "France won the FIFA World Cup 2018"
2. print("France" in sentence)
```

Output:

```
True
```

The following example shows that when a substring is not found inside another string, the "in" operator returns false.

Script 25:

```
1. sentence = "France won the FIFA World Cup 2018"
2. print("England" in sentence)
```

Output:

```
False
```

4.7.6. Splitting a String

In Python, the split() function is used to split a string. The character in the string that you want to use as a delimiter for splitting a string is passed as a parameter to the split() function. If you do not pass any argument value to the split() function, the string will be split() by empty spaces as shown below:

Script 26:

```
1. sentence = "France won the FIFA World Cup 2018"
2. print(sentence.split())
```

Output:

```
['France', 'won', 'the', 'FIFA', 'World', 'Cup', '2018']
```

> **Further Readings – Regex and Python String Functions**
>
> To read further about how to use regular expressions for text cleaning and manipulation, take a look at the official documentation for regular expressions in Python:
> https://docs.python.org/3/library/re.html
>
> Similarly, to study more about Python's default string functions, take a look at the official documentation for Python string functions:
> https://docs.python.org/2.5/lib/string-methods.html

Exercise 4.1

Consider the following sentence:

```
sentence = "Nick's car was sold for $ 1500".
```

Perform the following tasks on the above sentence:

1. Replace special characters with empty spaces

2. Remove multiple empty spaces and replace them by a single space

3. Remove any single character

4. Convert the text to all lower case

5. Split the text to individual words

Exercise 4.2

Question 1:

To remove special characters from a string, which regular expression can be used?

    A. re.sub(r"[^\w]", "", sentence, flags =re.I)

    B. re.sub(r"[^a-zA-z0-9]", "", sentence, flags =re.I)

    C. Both A and B

    D. None of the Above

Question 2:

To find if a string exists in another substring, we can use:

    A. contains operator

    B. exist operator

    C. in operator

    D. substring operator

Question 3:

Which regular expression is used to match any string with at least one character?

    A. re.match(r".*", sentence)

    B. re.match(r".+", sentence)

    C. re.match(r".-", sentence)

    D. re.match(r"./", sentence)

Common NLP Tasks

5.1. Introduction

In the previous chapter, you studied some text cleaning and manipulation techniques. In addition to text cleaning, you often need to perform additional preprocessing tasks before using your text to develop NLP applications. For instance, you might want to remove stop words from a text, tokenize longer sentences into individual words, or find the parts of speech tags for all the words.

In this chapter, you will see some of the most common NLP tasks that you often need to perform in order to preprocess your text.

5.2. Tokenization

Tokenization refers to dividing a document into a list of individual words. You might want to remove stop words or find parts of speech tags for individual words in your sentence. To do so, you will first need to divide the sentence into individual words.

In order to tokenize text, you can use the **word_tokenize()** method from the NLTK library to tokenize text.

The NLTK (Natural Language Toolkit) library is one of the most commonly used libraries for NLP. Execute the following command on the command terminal to install the NLTK library.

```
$pip install nltk
```

Here is an example of tokenization with NLTK.

Script 1:

```
1.  import nltk
2.  text = "Hello, this is a very useful book for deep
    learning"
3.  tokens = nltk.word_tokenize(text)
4.  print(tokens)
```

The **word_tokenize()** method accepts string text as a parameter and returns a list of individual words in the string that is passed as a parameter. Here is the output of the above script:

Output:

```
['Hello', ',', 'this', 'is', 'a', 'very', 'useful', 'book',
'for', 'deep', 'learning']
```

5.3. Stop Word Removal

Stop words are commonly used words such as a, is, am, it, he, and she. These words may or may not play any role while training the deep learning algorithms, depending upon the task at hand. Sometimes, stop words are removed altogether from the dataset.

To remove stop words, you have to first download a list of stop words from NLTK. Next, you need to tokenize your text and then check if the word exists in the stop words list. If the word is found in the stop word list, ignore that word. Or else, add the word in the list of words that are not stop words.

The following script shows how you can remove stop words from a dataset.

Script 2:

```
1.  from nltk.corpus import stopwords
2.  nltk.download('stopwords')
3.  from nltk.tokenize import word_tokenize
4.
5.  text = "Hello, this is a very useful book for deep
    learning"
6.  word_tokens = word_tokenize(text)
7.
8.  text_without_stopwords = [word for word in word_tokens if
    not word in stopwords.words()]
9.
10. print(" ".join(text_without_stopwords))
```

Output:

```
Hello, useful book deep learning
```

5.4. Stemming and Lemmatization

Stemming refers to reducing a word to its stem form. For instance, the stem of the word computer, computed, and computing is "comput."

To perform stemming, you can use the **PorterStemmer** object from the **nltk.stem** module. The word that you want to apply stemming on is passed to the **stem()** function of the **PorterStemmer** object.

Here is an example of how you can perform stemming with the NLTK library.

Script 3:

```
1.  from nltk.stem import PorterStemmer
2.  words = ["Compute", "Computer", "Computing", "Computed",
    "Computes"]
3.  ps =PorterStemmer()
4.  for word in words :
5.      stem=ps.stem(word)
6.      print(stem)
```

Output:

```
comput
comput
comput
comput
comput
```

Lemmatization refers to reducing a word to its root form, as found in the dictionary. Lemmatization is different from stemming. In stemming, a word is reduced to its root form even if the root has no meaning. On the other hand, in lemmatization, a word is reduced to its meaningful representation, as found in a dictionary.

To perform lemmatization, you can use the **WordNet-Lemmatizer** object from the **nltk.stem** module. The word that you want to apply stemming on is passed to the **lemmatize()** function of the **WordNetLemmatizer** object.

The following script shows how to perform lemmatization using the NLTK library.

Script 4:

```
1.  import nltk
2.  from nltk.stem import   WordNetLemmatizer
3.  wordnet_lemmatizer = WordNetLemmatizer()
4.  words = ["acts", "acted", "smiles", "smile"]
5.
6.  for word in words :
7.      lemma = wordnet_lemmatizer.lemmatize(word)
8.      print(lemma)
```

Output:

```
act
acted
smile
smile
```

5.5. Parts of Speech Tagging and Named Entity Recognition

You often need to find parts of speech of the words in a sentence. For instance, you may want to find if a word is a noun, pronoun, or a person, etc. With NLTK, you can easily find if a word is a verb, noun, pronoun, or any other parts of speech.

To find parts of speech and named entities, you can use the **pos_tags** functionality from the NLTK module. You have to pass the tokenlzed words to the **pos_tags** function. Here is an example.

The following script shows how to do parts of speech tagging using NLTK.

Script 5:

```
1. import nltk
2. text = "This is a very useful book for NLP in English by
   Usman Malik"
3. tokens = nltk.word_tokenize(text)
4. nltk.pos_tag(tokens)
```

In the output below, you can see the words and the abbreviations for the POS tags. For example, NNP refers to proper pronoun singular.

Output:

```
[('This', 'DT'),
 ('is', 'VBZ'),
 ('a', 'DT'),
 ('very', 'RB'),
 ('useful', 'JJ'),
 ('book', 'NN'),
 ('for', 'IN'),
 ('NLP', 'NNP'),
 ('in', 'IN'),
 ('English', 'NNP'),
 ('by', 'IN'),
 ('Usman', 'NNP'),
 ('Malik', 'NNP')]
```

To see the detailed names for the POS tags, check this link:

https://bit.ly/2N7qPRV

Wikipedia defines named entities as:

"a **named entity** is a real-world object, such as persons, locations, organizations, products, etc., that can be denoted with a proper name."

In parts of speech tags, named entities are denoted by NNP, i.e., proper noun singular. In the previous example, you can see that "NLP," "English," "Usman," and "Malik" are assigned NNP tags since they are named entities.

Let's see another example of named entities. This time, we will use the **SpaCy** library.

Run the following command on the terminal to download SpaCy:

```
$pip install spacy
```

Execute the following script to download the **SpaCy** library for natural language processing. Look at the following script:

Script 6:

```
1.  import spacy
2.  nlp = spacy.load("en_core_web_sm")
3.  doc1 = nlp("Eifel Tower is located in Paris")
4.
5.  for word in doc1:
6.      print(word.text,  word.pos_)
```

SpaCy has several language models in different languages. We will use the small English model. The model can be loaded via the **load()** method.

Next, to create a **SpaCy** text object, you need to pass the text string as a parameter to the model object. In the above script, we create a **doc1** object. Next, you can iterate on the model and use text and pos_attributes to display the text and parts of speech tag for each word.

Here is the output of the above script. You can see that both "Eifel" and "Tower" are assigned proper pronoun tags since they are parts of a single word. Similarly, "Paris" has also been identified as a proper pronoun.

Output:

```
Eifel PROPN
Tower PROPN
is AUX
located VERB
in ADP
Paris PROPN
```

5.6. Semantic Text Similarity

Semantic similarity refers to the similarity in the meaning of different text documents. To find semantic similarity, you can again use the SpaCy library. The **similarity()** method returns semantic similarity between two documents. The method returns a value between 0 and 1, where 1 represents 100 percent similarity.

Script 7:

```
1.  import spacy
2.  nlp = spacy.load("en_core_web_sm")
3.
4.  doc1 = nlp("Cricket is a sport where a team has 11 players")
5.  doc2 = nlp("A football team consists of 11 players")
6.  doc1.similarity(doc2)
```

Output:

```
0.7681408983878834
```

The output of 76.81 percent shows that the two documents in Script 7 are almost similar.

5.7. Word Sense Disambiguation

A word can have different meanings in different contexts. For instance, when you say, "I live on the bank of a river," you are talking about the edge of the river. If you say "I withdrew some money from my bank," the word bank, in this context, refers to a place that manages money. The process of identifying the correct meaning of a word in a given context refers to word sense disambiguation.

To perform word sense disambiguation, you can use the **pywsd** library, which stands for "Python word sense disambiguation."

Execute the following script to install the **pywsd** library:

```
$pip install pywsd
```

The **disambiguate()** method of the library accepts a word and returns its id as located in the wordnet dictionary. To know more about wordnet, take a look at this link:

https://wordnet.princeton.edu/

Here is an example of word sense disambiguation using the **pywsd** library.

Script 8:

```
1. from pywsd import disambiguate
2. from nltk import sent_tokenize
3.
4. text= "I live on the bank of a river"
5. text2 = "I withdrew some money from my bank"
6. for sent in sent_tokenize(text):
7.     print (disambiguate(sent, prefersNone=True))
8.
9. for sent in sent_tokenize(text2):
10.     print (disambiguate(sent, prefersNone=True))
```

Output:

```
[('I', None), ('live', Synset('survive.v.01')), ('on', None),
('the', None), ('bank', Synset('bank.n.01')), ('of', None),
('a', None), ('river', Synset('river.n.01'))]
[('I', None), ('withdrew', Synset('withdraw.v.09')), ('some',
None), ('money', Synset('money.n.03')), ('from', None), ('my',
None), ('bank', Synset('savings_bank.n.02'))]
```

From the output, you can see that each word is assigned a synset value from the WordNet dictionary. Synset is basically a set of synonyms where nouns, verbs, adjectives, and adverbs are grouped into sets of cognitive synonyms (synsets), each expressing a distinct concept. In the above script, the first bank is assigned an id "bank.n.01" and the bank in the second sentence is assigned a synset id of "saving_bank.n.02."

Let's now see the definition of these ids. To do so, you can use the **WordNet** module from the **nltk.corpus library.**

Script 9:

```
1.  from nltk.corpus import wordnet
2.
3.  syns = wordnet.synsets("bank")
4.
5.  for ss in syns:
6.      print(ss, ss.definition())
```

Output:

```
Synset('bank.n.01') sloping land (especially the slope beside
a body of water)
Synset('depository_financial_institution.n.01') a financial
institution that accepts deposits and channels the money into
lending activities
Synset('bank.n.03') a long ridge or pile
Synset('bank.n.04') an arrangement of similar objects in a row
or in tiers
Synset('bank.n.05') a supply or stock held in reserve for
future use (especially in emergencies)
Synset('bank.n.06') the funds held by a gambling house or the
dealer in some gambling games
Synset('bank.n.07') a slope in the turn of a road or track;
the outside is higher than the inside in order to reduce the
effects of centrifugal force
Synset('savings_bank.n.02') a container (usually with a slot
in the top) for keeping money at home
```

From the definition of the ids, you can clearly see that the word bank in "bank of a river" is different (bank.n.01) compared to the word "savings_bank.n.02," which is a container to place money.

Further Readings – Common NLP Tasks

For more about synsets and wordnet: https://www.nltk.org/howto/wordnet.html

For more about spacy:
https://spacy.io/

To learn more about pywsd:
https://github.com/alvations/pywsd

Hands-on Time – Exercise

Now, it is your turn. Follow the instructions in **the exercises below** to check your understanding of common NLP tasks. The answers to these questions are given at the end of the book.

Exercise 5.1

Remove special characters and digits from the following text and then perform stop word removal and tokenize. Finally, print the output. You can take help from chapter 4 to remove special characters and digits.

Note: The following text is obtained from the first two paragraphs of the Wikipedia's article on Machine Learning:

```
1. text = """Machine learning (ML) is the study of computer
   algorithms that improve automatically through experience.
   [1]
2. It is seen as a subset of artificial intelligence. Machine
   learning algorithms build a mathematical model based on
   sample data,
3. known as "training data",
4. in order to make predictions or decisions without being
   explicitly programmed to do so.[2][3]:2 Machine learning
   algorithms are
5. used in a wide variety of applications, such as email
   filtering and computer vision, where it is difficult or
   infeasible to develop conventional algorithms to perform
   the needed tasks.
6.
7. Machine learning is closely related to computational
   statistics, which focuses on making predictions using
   computers.
8. The study of mathematical optimization delivers methods,
   theory and application domains to the field of machine
   learning.
9. Data mining is a related field of study, focusing on
   exploratory data analysis through unsupervised learning.
   [4][5]
10. In its application across business problems, machine
    learning is also referred to as predictive analytics."""
```

Exercise 5.2

Question 1:

Which NLTK function is used to divide a sentence into individual words?

    A. text_tokenize()

    B. word_tokenize()

    C. tokenize()

    D. None of the Above

Question 2:

Which POS tag represents named entities?

    A. NNP

    B. NP

    C. PP

    D. NE

Question 3:

Word sense disambiguation is used when:

    A. A word has the same meaning in multiple sentences

    B. A word has different meanings in multiple sentences

    C. A word is the opposite of another word

    D. None of the above

Importing Text Data from Various Sources

To develop NLP models, you need text. There are various sources to obtain textual data, for instance, plain text files, CSV and TSV files, databases, and even websites. It is important to understand how to import textual data from various sources.

In this chapter, you will see how to import textual data from different data sources. So, let's begin without much ado.

> **Requirements – Anaconda, Jupyter, and Pandas**
> - All the scripts in this chapter have been executed via Jupyter notebook. Therefore, you should have Jupyter notebook installed.
> - The Pandas library should also be installed before this chapter.

6.1. Reading Text Files

A text file is one of the most common sources of text. To read text from a text file, you do not need to download any library. You can simply open a file using the **open()** function by passing the path file to the function. To read text line by line, you can then call the **readlines()** function.

The following script reads the "simple_textfile.txt" file (you can find it in the *Resources/Datasets* folder). Next, each line of the text in the file is stored in the lines list. Finally, the length of the list is displayed.

Script 1:

```
1. with open("E:\Datasets\simple_textfile.txt") as f:
2.     lines = f.readlines()
3.
4. print(len(lines))
```

You can create a Pandas dataframe using a list of lines. To do so, you need to pass a Python dictionary where the key name is the column header while the value corresponds to the list of lines. Look at the following script:

Script 2:

```
1. import pandas as pd
2. sentence = pd.DataFrame({'Sentences':lines})
3. sentence.head()
```

Output:

	Sentences
0	In the early days, many language-processing sy...
1	\n
2	Since the so-called "statistical revolution"[1...
3	The machine-learning paradigm calls instead fo...
4	is a set of documents, possibly with human or ...

6.2. Reading CSV Files

Sometimes, your text is stored inside a CSV file column. A CSV file is a type of file where each line contains a single record, and all the columns are separated from each other via a comma.

You read CSV files using the **read_csv()** function of the Pandas dataframe, as shown below. The "yelp_reviews.csv" file is available in the *Resources/Datasets* folder.

Script 3:

```
1. import pandas as pd
2. patients_csv = pd.read_csv(r"E:\Datasets\yelp_reviews.
   csv", encoding = "utf-8")
3. patients_csv.head()
```

If you print the dataframe header, you should see that the header contains a column *Text* which contains reviews about different products.

Output:

	text	useful	funny	cool
Super simple place but amazing nonetheless. It...		0	0	0
Small unassuming place that changes their menu...		0	0	0
Lester's is located in a beautiful neighborhoo...		0	0	0
Love coming here. Yes the place always needs t...		0	0	0
Had their chocolate almond croissant and it wa...		0	0	0

6.3. Reading TSV Files

TSV files are similar to CSV files, but in a TSV file, the delimiter used to separate columns is a single tab. The **read_csv()** function can be used to read a TSV file. However, you have to pass "\t" as a value for the "sep" attribute, as shown below.

Note: You can find the "rt_review.tsv" file in the *Resources/ Datasets* folder.

Script 4:

```
1. import pandas as pd
2. patients_csv = pd.read_csv(r"E:\Datasets\rt_reviews.tsv",
   sep='\t')
3. patients_csv.head()
```

Output:

	PhraseId	SentenceId	Phrase	Sentiment
0	1	1	A series of escapades demonstrating the adage ...	1
1	2	1	A series of escapades demonstrating the adage ...	2
2	3	1	A series	2
3	4	1	A	2
4	5	1	series	2

6.4. Importing Data from Databases

Oftentimes, you need to import data from different databases in order to develop your NLP applications. In this section, you will see how to import data from various databases into a Python application.

6.4.1. Importing Data from SQL Server

To import data from Microsoft's SQL Server database, you need to first install the "pyodbc" module for Python. To do so, execute the following command on your command terminal.

```
$ pip install pyodbc
```

Next, you need to create a connection with your SQL server database. The **connect()** method of the "pyodbc" module can be used to create a connection. You have to pass the driver name, the server name, and the database name to the connect() method, as shown below.

Note: In order to run the following script, you need to create a *Hospital* database with a *Patients* table. Explaining how to create a database and tables is beyond the scope of this book.

Further Readings – CRUD Operations with SQL Server

To see how to create database and tables with SQL Server, take a look at this link: https://bit.ly/2XwEgAV

In the following script, we connect to the *Hospital* database.

Script 5:

```
1.  import pandas as pd
2.  import pyodbc
3.
4.  sql_conn = pyodbc.connect('DRIVER={ODBC Driver 17
    for SQL Server}; SERVER=DESKTOP-IIBLKH1\SQLEXPRESS;
    DATABASE=Hospital;  Trusted_Connection=yes')
```

Once the connection is established, you have to write an SQL SELECT query that fetches the desired record. The following SQL select query fetches all records from a *Patients* table. In a Pandas dataframe, the query and the connection object are passed to the **pd_read_sql()** function to store the records returned by the query. Finally, the dataframe header is printed to display the first five rows of the imported table.

Script 6:

```
1. query = "SELECT * FROM Patients;"
2. patients_data_ss = pd.read_sql(query, sql_conn)
3. patients_data_ss.head()
```

	Id	Name	Age	Gender	Nationality	Married	Comments
0	1	Rooney Moss	48	1	Peru	True	Maecenas iaculis aliquet diam. Sed diam lorem,...
1	2	Cole Gallegos	45	0	Mauritius	False	egestas, urna justo faucibus lectus, a sollici...
2	3	Dieter Glenn	67	1	Canada	True	nunc interdum feugiat. Sed nec metus facilisis...
3	4	Elton Durham	54	0	Congo (Brazzaville)	True	Nunc sollicitudin commodo ipsum. Suspendisse n...
4	5	Ashton Larson	88	1	Monaco	True	molestie dapibus ligula. Aliquam erat volutpat...

6.4.2. Importing Data from PostgreSQL

To import data from PostgreSQL, you will need to download the *SQLAlchemy* module. Execute the following pip statement to do so.

```
$ pip install SQLAlchemy
```

Next, you need to create an engine, which serves as a connection between the PostgreSQL server and the Python application. The following script shows how to create a connection engine. You need to replace your server and database name in the following script.

Script 7:

```
1. from sqlalchemy import create_engine
2. engine = create_engine('postgresql://postgres:abc123@
   localhost:5432/Hospital')
```

To store the records returned by the query in a Pandas dataframe, the query and the connection object is passed to the **pd_read_sql()** function of the Pandas dataframe. Finally, the dataframe header is printed to display the first five rows of the imported table.

Script 8:

```
1. import pandas as pd
2. patients_data_psg =pd.read_sql_query('select * from
   "Patients"',con=engine)
3. patients_data_psg.head()
```

Output:

	id	name	age	gender	nationality	married	comments
0	1	Adrian Burns	22	1	Bermuda	True	dolor, nonummy ac, feugiat non, lobortis quis,...
1	2	George Padilla	55	1	Paraguay	False	Suspendisse aliquet. sem ut cursus luctus. ips...
2	3	Stephen Marks	12	0	Western Sahara	True	egestas. Aliquam nec enim. Nunc ut erat. Sed n...
3	4	Rahim York	74	1	Thailand	False	consectetuer euismod est arcu ac orci. Ut semp...
4	5	Edward Medina	61	1	Svalbard and Jan Mayen Islands	True	In faucibus. Morbi vehicula. Pellentesque tinc...

You can also print a single comment from the comment column, as shown below:

Script 9:

```
patients_data_psg["comments"][0]
```

Don't worry if the comment doesn't make any sense. This is just dummy text obtained from lorem ipsum.

Output:

```
'dolor, nonummy ac, feugiat non, lobortis quis, pede.
Suspendisse dui. Fusce diam nunc, ullamcorper eu, euismod ac,
fermentum vel, mauris. Integer sem elit, pharetra ut, pharetra
sed, hendrerit a, arcu. Sed et libero. Proin mi. Aliquam
gravida mauris ut mi. Duis risus odio, auctor vitae, aliquet
nec, imperdiet nec, leo.'
```

> **Further Readings – CRUD Operations with PostgreSQL**
> To see how to create database and tables with PostgreSQL, take a look at this link: https://bit.ly/2XyJr3f

6.4.3. Importing Data from SQLite

To import data from an SQLite database, you do not need any external module. You can use the default *sqlite3* module.

The first step is to connect to an SQLite database. To do so, you can use the **connect()** method of the sqlite3 module, as shown below:

Script 10:

```
1.  import sqlite3
2.  import pandas as pd
3.  # Create your connection.
4.  cnx = sqlite3.connect('E:/Hospital.db')
```

Next, you can call the pd_**read_sql()** function of the Pandas dataframe and pass it to the SELECT query and the database connection. Finally, the dataframe header is printed to display the first five rows of the imported table.

Script 11:

```
1.  patients_data_sl = pd.read_sql_query("SELECT * FROM
    Patients", cnx)
2.  patients_data_sl.head()
```

	Id	Name	Age	Gender	Nationality	Married	Comments
0	1	Melvin Moreno	89	0	Palau	True	nunc, ullamcorper eu, euismod ac, fermentum ve...
1	2	Nissim Erickson	73	1	Curaçao	False	Mauris blandit enim consequat purus. Maecenas ...
2	3	Vincent Morton	77	1	Palau	True	aliquam iaculis, lacus pede sagittis augue, eu...
3	4	Erasmus Browning	51	1	Virgin Islands, British	False	Nulla tempor augue ac ipsum. Phasellus vitae m...
4	5	Elton Osborne	14	0	Dominican Republic	True	Mauris vel turpis. Aliquam adipiscing lobortis...

> **Further Readings – CRUD Operations with SQLite**
> To see how to create database and tables with SQLite, take a look at this link: https://bit.ly/2BAXZXL

6.5. Scraping Data from Twitter

Oftentimes, the data is not available in the form of text files or databases. You have to scrape data directly from different websites. Some websites provide APIs that you can use to scrape data from those websites. For the websites that do not provide any, you have to use Scrapy (https://scrapy.org/) or other third-party modules.

In this section, you will see how to scrape data from Twitter using Python's *tweepy* module. The first thing that you have to do is install the *tweepy* module. To do so, execute the following script on your command terminal.

```
$ pip install tweepy
```

Before you can scrape tweets from Twitter using the *tweepy* module, you need to create a Twitter's Developer Account. Click this link to create a developer account: https://developer.twitter.com/en.

6.5.1. Creating a New Twitter Application

After creating your Twitter developer account, you need to create a Twitter application.

To do so, login to your developer account. Go to this link: https://developer.twitter.com/en/apps and then on the top right, click *Create an app* button.

Next, you have to enter the App Name, Website URL, and Application Description on the presented form. My application has been named *twitter-scraping-xyz* for the sake of this tutorial. For the website URL, you can add any place holder name as well. I used *www.google.com* for the website URL. Add a brief description for the app. Next, at the bottom, click the *Create* button. Leave the rest of the fields blank. They are not necessary.

6.5.2. Getting API Keys and Access Tokens

You will need consumer API keys and Access tokens to connect your Twitter server with Python. To do this, go to the application page. Next, at the top, you click on the *Keys and tokens* menu. On this page, both the API Key and API Secret Key can be seen. Next, click on *Create* for the Access Token and Access Token Secret.

6.5.3. Scraping Tweets from Twitter

Now you have everything that you need to scrape tweets from Twitter. Store the API Key, API Secret, Access Token, and Access Token Secret in Python variables, as shown below:

Note: Your keys will be different than the ones mentioned below:

Script 12:

```
1. import tweepy
2. import re
3.
4. from tweepy import OAuthHandler
5.
6. api_key = 'D5CvS7MrSfSoigFQFkQ5sioi4'
7. api_sec =
   'ci9IHZPJ218oX4rIolOzv359sq7iQ5vPVGuVHJW96IWIT3nyzD'
8. acc_tok =
   '165879850-d6GPXrp2nhM6qJG2lKleOcCJSZRhED435N8sgxD8'
9. acc_tok_sec
   ='kQsvtXf5pajEiqT6L2HOpxN9BYakrWDOHmsMKo0C6j18U'
```

Next, you need to create an object of the "OAuthHandler" class by passing the API Key and API Secret to the class constructor. After that, you need to call the **set_access_token()** method of the object and pass it your Access Token and Access Token Secret. These two steps are performed in the following script:

Script 13:

```
1. api_handler = OAuthHandler(api_key, api_sec)
2. api_handler.set_access_token(acc_tok, acc_tok_sec)
```

To scrape the tweets, you first need to create the API object. After that, you need to define the keyword that you want to use to search tweets. Finally, call the **tweepy.Cursor()** method to retrieve tweets, as shown below.

The following script retrieves 200 tweets that contain the keyword "facebook." The tweets are appended in a list.

Script 14:

```
1.  api_object = tweepy.API(api_handler, timeout=10)
2.
3.  tweets_list = []
4.
5.  search_string = 'facebook'
6.
7.  cursor = tweepy.Cursor(api_object.search, q=search_
    string+" -filter:retweets",lang='en',result_type='recent').
    items(200)
8.
9.  for single_tweet in cursor:
10.     tweets_list.append(single_tweet.text)
```

The list of tweets is then converted to Pandas dataframe, and the header of the dataframe is printed via the following script.

Script 15:

```
1.  tweets = pd.DataFrame({'Tweets':tweets_list})
2.  tweets.head()
```

Output:

	Tweets
0	If you follow anyone associated with our site ...
1	@bluehatman Sky News Australia is the one I fo...
2	Facebook is introducing a new tool to help use...
3	America us \nWhite Cop kneels on arrested &amp...
4	@mariafeldman14 @mattickus @SilasATaylor @NYCM...

Further Readings – Scraping Facebook Data

To see how to scrape data from Facebook, refer to this article: https://bit.ly/2BsvACR.

Hands-on Time – Exercise

Now, it is your turn. Follow the instructions in **the exercises below** to check your understanding of importing text data from various sources. The answers to these questions are given at the end of the book.

Exercise 6.1

Question 1:

Which delimiter is used to read the TSV file with the Pandas read_csv method?

    A. sep ='tab'

    B. sep = ' '

    C. sep ='\t'

    D. None of the Above

Question 2:

Which Python module is used to import data from SQL Server?

    A. SqlAlchemy

    B. pyodbc

    C. sqlite3

    D. None of the Above

Question 3:

Which function is used to convert a database table to a Pandas dataframe?

    A. pd.read_sql_query

    B. pd.read_sql

    C. pd.read_csv

    D. pd.read_tsv

Exercise 6.2

In the *data folder of the book resources*, you will find a file CSV *airline_review*. Read the CSV file, and print the first five reviews. You can use the head method of the Pandas dataframe for that purpose.

7

Word Embeddings: Converting Words to Numbers

7.1. Word Embeddings: What and Why?

Statistical algorithms like machine learning and deep learning work with numbers. To apply statistical algorithms on text, you need to convert text to numbers. For instance, you cannot add two words *apples* and *oranges.* You need to convert text to numbers in order to apply mathematical operations on words.

The process of converting text to numbers, mostly in the form of vectors, is called word embeddings. In this chapter, you will see some of the most common approaches for word embeddings. The following are some of the most common word embedding approaches:

1. Bag of Words

2. N-Grams

3. TFIDF Approach

4. Word2Vec

In this chapter, you will see the theory behind these approaches, and you will also see how to implement these approaches with Python.

7.2. Bag of Words Approach

Bag of Words (BOW) is one of the most familiar and oldest approaches for converting words to numbers.

The bag of words approach is extremely simple. Let me explain it with the help of an example.

Suppose you have a corpus with the following sentences:

```
1.  corpus = ["He likes to watch movies",
2.             "French movies are good to watch movies",
3.             "Do you like French movies?"]
```

The above corpus contains three sentences. The bag of words approach works in the following steps:

1. Create a dictionary containing all the unique words in all the documents in the corpus. The dictionary for our corpus will look like this. You can see that there are 11 unique words in the dictionary.

He	likes	to	watch	movies	French	are	good	Do	you	like

2. Assign an index number to every unique word in the dictionary created in step 1. You can assign any index number. Index numbers should preferably start from 0. Let's suppose we assign the following index numbers to the words in the dictionary.

He	likes	to	watch	movies	French	are	good	Do	you	like
4	6	8	9	7	2	0	3	1	10	5

3. For each sentence or document in the original corpus, create an N-dimensional vector of all 0s, where N is the number of words in the dictionary that contains the vocabulary of the corpus. In our case, we will create three 11 dimensional vectors with all 0s.

4. For each word in the original sentence, if the word exists in the dictionary of unique words, add the frequency of the word in the sentence to the corresponding 11-dimensional vector at the index, as mentioned in the dictionary of unique words.

   For example, the first sentence in our corpus is: "He likes to watch movies." The index of the first word "He" as per the dictionary of unique words is 4. Since the word "He" occurs only once in the sentence, in the 11-dimensional vector for the sentence, a 1 will be added at the 4th index.

   Similarly, the indexes for the words "likes to watch movies" are 6, 8, 9, and 7. Therefore, 1 will be added to these indexes. The final bag of words vector for the sentence "He likes to watch movies" will be: [0 0 0 0 1 0 1 1 1 1 0].

   Remember that the index number starts from 0. Therefore, the 4th index will actually be located at the 5th position in the BOW vector.

   Similarly, for the sentence "French movies are good to watch movies," the BOW vectors will look like this:

   [[1 0 1 1 0 0 0 2 1 1 0]]

   In the above vector, you can see 2 at the seventh index. This is because the seventh index is reserved for the word "movies" in our dictionary. And since the word "movies" occurs twice in the sentence, hence the digit 2 is added to the 7th index.

Let's now see how you can create a bag of words model with Python's SKlearn library.

To create a bag of words model with the SKlearn library, you can use the **CountVectorizer** class from the **sklearn.feature_ extraction.text module.** You need to pass the corpus of the sentence to the **fit()** method, as shown below. Next, to see the vocabulary of unique words, you can use the **vocabulary_** attribute, as shown below:

Script 1:

```
4.  corpus = ["He likes to watch movies",
5.             "French movies are good to watch movies",
6.             "Do you like French movies?"]
7.
8.
9.  from sklearn.feature_extraction.text import
    CountVectorizer
10. bog_vectorizer = CountVectorizer()
11.
12. bog_vectorizer.fit(corpus)
13. print(bog_vectorizer.vocabulary_)
```

In the following output, you can see the unique words in the corpus along with the indexes assigned to the words.

Output:

```
{'he': 4, 'likes': 6, 'to': 8, 'watch': 9, 'movies': 7,
'french': 2, 'are': 0, 'good': 3, 'do': 1, 'you': 10, 'like':
5}
```

The fit method only creates a dictionary of unique words along with the indexes. To convert text documents to a bag of words vector, you need to pass the sentences to the **transform()** method of the **CountVectorizer** object, as shown below. To display the vectors, you can call the **toArray()** method on each individual vector.

Script 2:

```
1. bog_vectors =  bog_vectorizer.transform(corpus)
2. for i in range(len(corpus)):
3.     print(corpus[i],"-->",bog_vectors[i].toarray())
```

Output:

```
He likes to watch movies --> [[0 0 0 0 1 0 1 1 1 1 0]]
French movies are good to watch movies --> [[1 0 1 1 0 0 0 2 1
1 0]]
Do you like French movies? --> [[0 1 1 0 0 1 0 1 0 0 1]]
```

You can also remove stop words while creating a **CountVectorizer** object. You can pass a list of stop words to the "stop_words" attribute. The stop words passed in the list are not added to the vocabulary dictionary. Here is an example.

Script 3:

```
1. from sklearn.feature_extraction.text import
   CountVectorizer
2. bog_vectorizer = CountVectorizer(stop_words=["to", "you",
   "are", "he", "do"])
3.
4. bog_vectorizer.fit(corpus)
5. print(bog_vectorizer.vocabulary_)
```

Output:

```
{'likes': 3, 'watch': 5, 'movies': 4, 'french': 0, 'good': 1,
'like': 2}
```

The following script prints the word bag of words vectors without the stop words.

Script 4:

```
1. bog_vectors =  bog_vectorizer.transform(corpus)
2. for i in range(len(corpus)):
3.     print(corpus[i],"-->",bog_vectors[i].toarray())
```

Output:

```
He likes to watch movies --> [[0 0 0 1 1 1]]
French movies are good to watch movies --> [[1 1 0 0 2 1]]
Do you like French movies? --> [[1 0 1 0 1 0]]
```

One of the main advantages of the bag of words approach is that it doesn't require a large amount of data to train. In addition, the bag of words approach is easy to understand.

A major downside to the BOW approach is that in the case of a large corpus, the size of the dictionary increases exponentially, resulting in a sparse matrix. For example, if your corpus has ten thousand unique words, each document in the corpus will be represented by a ten thousand-dimensional vector. Even if the sentence contains 20 words, it has to be represented by a 10-dimensional vector, resulting in the loss of huge space.

Another matter of concern with the bag of words approach is that it fails to retain any context information. For instance, the sentences "John likes cats" and "Cats likes John" will have the same BOW vector. The context information can be partially retained via the N-Grams approach.

7.3. N-Grams Approach

In the N-Grams approach, instead of creating a dictionary of unique words, a dictionary of unique n-grams is created where N can be any number. For example, for the sentence "He likes to eat mangoes," a dictionary 2-grams (also known as bigrams) will be:

He likes	likes to	to eat	eat mangoes

Similarly, 3- grams (also known as trigrams) will look like this.

He likes to	Likes to eat	To eat mangoes

The rest of the process is similar to the BOW approach.

Let's see how to create N-Grams with Sklearn. To do so, you can again use the **CountVectorizer** class from the **sklearn.feature_extraction.text** module. To specify a range of N-Grams, you can use the **ngram_range** attribute. It accepts a tuple with two numbers.

The first number is the lower bound for the n-grams, and the second number corresponds to the upper bound. In the following script, you will see how to create numeric vectors using the 2-grams approach.

Script 5:

```
1.  corpus = ["He likes to watch movies",
2.              "French movies are good to watch movies",
3.              "Do you like French movies?"]
4.
5.
6.  from sklearn.feature_extraction.text import
    CountVectorizer
7.  ng_vectorizer = CountVectorizer(ngram_range=(2,2))
8.
9.  ng_vectorizer.fit(corpus)
10. print(ng_vectorizer.vocabulary_)
```

The output shows the dictionary containing the 2-grams for your input sentences. Like BOW, an index is assigned to each 2-gram.

Output:

```
{'he likes': 4, 'likes to': 6, 'to watch': 8, 'watch movies':
9, 'french movies': 2, 'movies are': 7, 'are good': 0, 'good
to': 3, 'do you': 1, 'you like': 10, 'like french': 5}
```

Next, you can convert your input sentences into N-grams using the **transform()** method of the **CountVectorizer** as shown below:

Script 6:

```
1. ng_vectors =  ng_vectorizer.transform(corpus)
2. for i in range(len(corpus)):
3.     print(corpus[i],"-->",ng_vectors[i].toarray())
```

Output:

```
He likes to watch movies --> [[0 0 0 0 1 0 1 0 1 1 0]]
French movies are good to watch movies --> [[1 0 1 1 0 0 0 1 1
1 0]]
Do you like French movies? --> [[0 1 1 0 0 1 0 0 0 0 1]]
```

The advantages of the N-grams approach are similar to the Bag of Words approach. In addition, with the N-grams approach, you can retain some of the context information.

One of the main downsides of the N-grams approach is this approach is less suitable for learning phrases that are long.

7.4. TF-IDF Approach

The TF-IDF approach is similar to the bag of words approach. However, unlike the bag of words, the resultant numeric vector contains TF-IDF values for the words in a sentence instead of the frequency of occurrence.

The term TF refers to term frequency, whereas the term IDF refers to inverse document frequency.

The term frequency is easy to calculate:

TF = The number of times a term appears in a document.

IDF, on the other hand, is calculated as:

$$IDF = \ln\left(\frac{total\ number\ of\ documents + 1}{documents\ containing\ the\ term + 1}\right) + 1$$

The idea behind calculating TF-IDF is that the words that appear more in a particular document and less in all the documents are unique, and thus should be given higher weightage compared to the words that are common and occur in all the documents.

Let's try to find IDF values with examples. Suppose we have the following corpus:

```
1.  corpus = ["He likes to watch movies",
2.              "French movies are good to watch movies",
3.              "Do you like French movies?"]
```

Let's try to find the IDF value for the word *Likes*. The word *Likes*:

$$IDF\ (likes) = \ln\left(\frac{3+1}{1+1}\right) + 1$$

$$IDF\ (likes) = \ln(2) + 1$$

$$IDF\ (likes) = 1.693$$

This log value can also be used. However, Sklearn uses normalized TF-IDF values. The following formula is used to calculate the final normalized TF-IDF value for a word in a particular document. Here, n is the total number of words in a document.

$$Norm(TFIDF) = \frac{idf(word)}{\sqrt{(sqr(idf(word1) + sqr(idf(word2)...+sqr(idf(wordn))}}$$

Suppose the stop words "He" and "to" are removed, and we are left with three words in the first document, i.e., "likes," "watch," and "movies." The final normalized TF-IDF value for the word *likes* in the first sentence can be calculated as:

$$\text{Norm(TFIDF(likes))} = \frac{idf(likes)}{\sqrt{(sqr(idf(likes)+sqr(idf(watch)+sqr(idf(movies))}}$$

$$\text{Norm(TFIDF(likes))} = \frac{1.693}{\sqrt{(2.85+1+1.63)}}$$

$$\text{Norm(TFIDF(likes))} = 0.72$$

The final normalized TF-IDF value for the word *likes* is 0.72.

Let's now see how you can develop a TF-IDF model using the SKlearn library. To do so, you can use the **TfIdfVectorizer** class from the **sklearn.feature_extraction.text**. The process is the same. First, you have to call the **fit() method** and then the **transform()** method on the corpus. Also, you can pass **"stop_words = 'english'"** as an attribute to automatically remove stop words from your text. The first step to create a vocabulary dictionary containing unique words in the corpus is shown below:

Script 7:

```
4.  corpus = ["He likes to watch movies",
5.             "French movies are good to watch movies",
6.             "Do you like French movies?"]
7.
8.
9.  from sklearn.feature_extraction.text import TfidfVectorizer
10. tfidf_vectorizer = TfidfVectorizer(stop_words='english')
11.
12. tfidf_vectorizer.fit(corpus)
13. print(tfidf_vectorizer.vocabulary_)
```

Output:

```
{'likes': 3, 'watch': 5, 'movies': 4, 'french': 0, 'good': 1,
'like': 2}
```

Next, you can use the **toarray()** method to print the TF-IDF value for all the documents in your corpus.

Script 8:

```
1. tfidf_vectors = tfidf_vectorizer.transform(corpus)
2. for i in range(len(corpus)):
3.     print(corpus[i],"-->",tfidf_vectors[i].toarray())
```

Output:

```
He likes to watch movies --> [[0.          0.          0.
0.72033345 0.42544054 0.54783215]]
French movies are good to watch movies --> [[0.40352536
0.53058735 0.          0.          0.62674687 0.40352536]]
Do you like French movies? --> [[0.54783215 0.
0.72033345 0.          0.42544054 0.          ]]
```

Let's print the TF-IDF value for each unique word in the corpus.

Script 9:

```
1. df1=pd.DataFrame(tfidf_vectors.todense(),columns=['french',
   'good', 'like', 'likes', 'movies', 'watch'])
2. df1
```

Output:

	french	good	like	likes	movies	watch
0	0.000000	0.000000	0.000000	0.720333	0.425441	0.547832
1	0.403525	0.530587	0.000000	0.000000	0.626747	0.403525
2	0.547832	0.000000	0.720333	0.000000	0.425441	0.000000

From the above output, you can see that in the first document, the final normalized TF-IDF value for the word *likes* is 0.7203, which is similar to what we calculated manually.

Though the TF-IDF embeddings generally work better than Bag of Words, it has the same limitations as Bag of Words and N-Grams. The size of the TF-IDF vectors is huge, and it is also not possible to retain the context information.

This is where the Word2Vec word embeddings come to play.

7.5. Word2Vec

Word2Vec is a neural network-based technique where each word in a text document is represented via a dense vector. The vectors for the words that occur in the same context have similar dimensions values. The Word2Vec approach not only saves space but also captures context. Word2Vec model is developed at Google by Mikolov et al. (https://bit.ly/2UvbL4t).

With Word2Vec techniques, you can achieve amazing performance on various NLP tasks. For instance, with embedding vectors for the words king, man, woman, and queen, you can perform tasks like:

King – man + women = queen.

There are two types of word2vec operations: Continuous Bag of Words (CBOW) and Skip Gram Model. In CBOW models, the input words are surrounding words, and the output is the word that is in between the surrounded words. For instance, if you have a sentence "The quick brown fox jumps over the lazy dog," for CBOW model, one of the inputs will be "quick fox" and the output will be "brown." For the skipgram model, the input is "brown," and the output is "quick fox." An overview of the word2vec model is shown in the following figure.

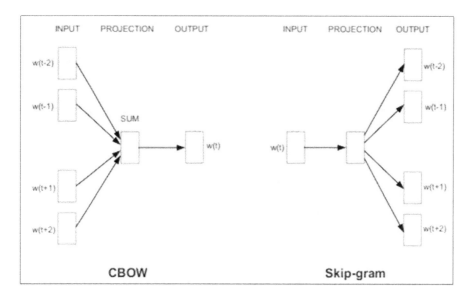

The word2vec models are trained via a shallow neural network with one layer. The weights of the nodes or cells in the shallow layer are basically the embeddings for words. The words that exist together in the text will have similar embeddings.

There are two options. Either you can use pretrained Word2Vec word embeddings, or you can create your own custom word embeddings. In this section, we will see both approaches.

The CBOW mode is the most commonly used Word2Vec model. In the following sections, you will see how to create a CBOW Word2Vec model.

Creating Custom Word2Vec Word Embeddings

Various libraries exist that can be used to create a Word2Vec model. We will be using the Gensim (https://bit.ly/2BLR6Tg) library in this chapter to create Word2Vec models.

For installing the Gensim library, execute the following command:

Script 10:

```
$ pip install gensim
```

To create word embeddings with Genism, you need a text corpus. The "simple_textfile.txt" in the *Resources/Datasets* folder contains some random text, which we will be using to create a Word2Vec model. The following script opens the text file and reads its text.

Script 11:

```
1.  # Open a file: file
2.  file = open("E:\Datasets\simple_textfile.txt",mode='r')
3.
4.  corpus = file.read()
5.
6.  file.close()
```

Next, we perform some preprocessing on the text and remove all the special characters and numbers from the text. The empty spaces are also removed. The preprocessing script is as follows:

Script 12:

```
1.  import re
2.  processed_corpus = corpus.lower()
3.  processed_corpus = re.sub('[^a-zA-Z]', ' ', processed_
    corpus)
4.  processed_corpus = re.sub(r'\s+', ' ', processed_corpus)
```

The following script removes all the stop words from the corpus.

Script 13:

```
1.  import nltk
2.
3.  all_sentences = nltk.sent_tokenize(processed_corpus)
4.
5.  all_tokens = [nltk.word_tokenize(sent) for sent in all_
    sentences]
6.
7.  # Removing Stop Words
8.  from nltk.corpus import stopwords
9.  for i in range(len(all_tokens)):
10.     all_tokens[i] = [w for w in all_tokens[i] if w not in
    stopwords.words('english')]
```

To create Word2Vec embeddings, you can use the *Word2Vec* object from the *gensim.models* library. The tokenized list of words is passed to the constructor of the Word2Vec object. The size of the embedding vector is passed to the size attribute. Finally, we want that only those words are included in the embeddings that exist at least twice in the corpus.

The following script creates word embeddings using the text in the "simple_textfile.txt" in the *Resources/Datasets* folder.

Script 14:

```
1.  from gensim.models import Word2Vec
2.  custom_embeddings = Word2Vec(all_tokens, size = 50, min_
    count=2)
```

Next, to see word embeddings for a particular word, you can use the "wv" attribute and pass it the word for which you want to see the embeddings. The following script prints the embeddings for the word "language."

Script 15:

```
1.  embedding = custom_embeddings.wv['language']
2.  print(embedding)
```

Output:

```
[-0.00426598  0.0066667  -0.00994872 -0.0018594  -0.00368378
-0.00152758
 -0.00074282  0.00785413 -0.00063565  0.00349408  0.00979154
-0.00473177
  0.00720627 -0.00183818 -0.00537117  0.00785426  0.00251265
0.00769123
 -0.00811501 -0.00216821 -0.00799533  0.00863134 -0.00185704
0.00969618
  0.0028168  -0.00972727  0.00881161  0.00715959  0.00634548
0.00720468
  0.00580982  0.00541707  0.00326962  0.00124786 -0.00173341
-0.00210726
  0.00082567  0.00168776  0.00956614  0.007015    -0.00264531
-0.00101851
 -0.00378467 -0.0045118   0.00485406  0.00942281 -0.00058634
0.00399187
 -0.00708318 -0.00132198]
```

If you want to see the words that have embeddings similar to the word "processing," you can use the "wv.most_similar()" method as shown below:

Script 16:

```
1. embedding = custom_embeddings.wv.most_similar("processing")
2. print(embedding)
```

You can see the word processing is similar to "research," "words," etc. based on the text in the corpus used to create these embeddings.

Output:

```
[('research', 0.23508717119693756), ('words',
0.20266640186309814), ('g', 0.2025955319404602), ('soft',
0.17397646605968475), ('accurate', 0.15688738226890564),
('simply', 0.1476944088935852), ('large',
0.13822558522224426), ('made', 0.1043497771024704), ('data',
0.08629055321216583), ('systems', 0.08272531628608704)]
```

You can call the "save()" method on the embedding object to save your word embeddings.

Script 17:

```
custom_embeddings.save("E:\Datasets\custom_embeddings.model")
```

Similarly, to load a saved word embedding object created via Genism, you need to call the "load()" method of the Word2Vec object as shown below:

```
1. custom_embeddings_loaded = Word2Vec.load("E:\Datasets\
   custom_embeddings.model")
2. embedding_loaded = custom_embeddings_loaded.wv['language']
3. print(embedding_loaded)
```

Output:

```
[-0.00426598  0.0066667  -0.00994872 -0.0018594  -0.00368378
-0.00152758
 -0.00074282  0.00785413 -0.00063565  0.00349408  0.00979154
-0.00473177
  0.00720627 -0.00183818 -0.00537117  0.00785426  0.00251265
0.00769123
 -0.00811501 -0.00216821 -0.00799533  0.00863134 -0.00185704
0.00969618
  0.0028168  -0.00972727  0.00881161  0.00715959  0.00634548
0.00720468
  0.00580982  0.00541707  0.00326962  0.00124786 -0.00173341
-0.00210726
  0.00082567  0.00168776  0.00956614  0.007015   -0.00264531
-0.00101851
 -0.00378467 -0.0045118   0.00485406  0.00942281 -0.00058634
0.00399187
 -0.00708318 -0.00132198]
```

7.6. **Pretrained Word Embeddings**

In addition to using custom word embeddings, you can use pretrained word embeddings from Stanford Glove (https://

stanford.io/2MJW98X) or Word2Vec from Google (https://bit.
ly/3hhD5Nk).

We will see how to load Stanford Glove 100-dimensional
pretrained word embeddings into our application. To do
so, you need to download the "glove.6B.100d.txt" from the
Stanford Glove online source (https://stanford.io/2MJW98X).

The following script shows how to convert the glove word
embedding text file into a format that can then be loaded to
create a Gensim Word2Vec model.

Script 18:

```
1.  from gensim.scripts.glove2word2vec import glove2word2vec
2.
3.  glove2word2vec(glove_input_file="E:\Datasets\glove.6B.100d.
    txt", word2vec_output_file="E:\Datasets\gensim_glove_vectors.
    txt")
```

The output shows that there are 4,00,000 words in the
Stanford Glove file that we downloaded, and each word is
represented by a 100-dimensional vector.

Output:

```
(400000, 100)
```

To create Gensim word embeddings, using "gensim_glove_
vectors.txt," execute the following script. The following script
also prints embeddings for the word "language."

Script 19:

```
1.  from gensim.models.keyedvectors import KeyedVectors
2.  glove_model = KeyedVectors.load_word2vec_format("E:\
    Datasets\gensim_glove_vectors.txt", binary=False)
3.  glove_model['language']
```

The 100-dimensional embedding for the word *language* is shown in the following output:

Output:

```
array([ 0.18519,  0.34111,  0.36097,  0.27093, -0.031335,
0.83923,
        -0.50534, -0.80062,  0.40695,  0.82488, -0.98239,
-0.6354,
        -0.21382,  0.079889, -0.29557,  0.17075,  0.17479,
-0.74214,
        -0.2677,  0.21074, -0.41795,  0.027713,  0.71123,
0.2063,
        -0.12266, -0.80088,  0.22942,  0.041037, -0.56901,
0.097472,
        -0.59139,  1.0524, -0.66803, -0.70471,  0.69757,
-0.11137,
        -0.27816,  0.047361,  0.020305, -0.184, -1.0254,
0.11297,
        -0.79547,  0.41642, -0.2508, -0.3188,  0.37044,
-0.26873,
        -0.36185, -0.096621, -0.029956,  0.67308,  0.53102,
0.62816,
        -0.11507, -1.5524, -0.30628, -0.4253,  1.8887,  0.3247,
        0.60202,  0.81163, -0.46029, -1.4061,  0.80229,
0.2019,
        0.60938,  0.063545,  0.21925, -0.043372, -0.36648,
0.61308,
        1.0207, -0.39014,  0.1717,  0.61272, -0.80342,
0.71295,
        -1.0938, -0.50546, -0.99668, -1.6701, -0.31804,
-0.62934,
        -2.0226,  0.79405, -0.16994, -0.37627,  0.57998,
0.16643,
        0.1356,  0.0943, -0.24154,  0.7123, -0.4201,  0.24735,
        -0.94449, -1.0794,  0.3413,  0.34704 ], dtype=float32)
```

To print similar words, you can use the "most_similar()" as shown below.

Script 20:

```
glove_model.most_similar('intelligence')
```

Output:

```
[('cia', 0.742180585861206),
 ('information', 0.7210196256637573),
 ('security', 0.6963101625442505),
 ('fbi', 0.6962289810180664),
 ('military', 0.6934822201728821),
 ('secret', 0.6893364191055298),
 ('counterterrorism', 0.6762625575065613),
 ('pentagon', 0.6651185154914856),
 ('defense', 0.6564568281173706),
 ('agents', 0.6406551599502563)]
```

Further Readings – Word Embeddings

To know more about word embeddings, see these resources:

https://bit.ly/2YaCaqt
https://bit.ly/3ORJeKx

Hands-on Time – Exercise

Now, it is your turn. Follow the instructions in **the exercises below** to check your understanding of word vectors and word embeddings. The answers to these questions are given at the end of the book.

Exercise 7.1

Question 1:

Which of the following is not a disadvantage of the Bag of Words and NGrams approaches?

A. Results in a huge sparse matrix

B. Context information is not retained

C. Requires a huge amount of data to train

D. None of the above

Question 2:

Which attribute is used to specify the range of N-Grams via Sklearn's CountVectorizer?

A. ngrams

B. ng_rage

C. ngrams_range

D. ngram_range

Question 3:

Suppose you develop a custom word2vec model "GensimModel" with Gensim. How will you display words similar to "Machine"?

A. GensimModel.wv.most_similar("Machine")

B. GensimModel.most_similar("Machine")

C. GensimModel.wv.similar("Machine")

D. GensimModel.similar("Machine")

Exercise 7.2

Using the following corpus, create bag of words and TF-IDF models without stop words. Display the original words and the bag of words and TF-IDF vectors:

```
1.  dataset = [
2.
3.      'This movie is excellent',
4.      'I loved the movie, it was fantastic',
5.      'The film is brilliant, you should watch',
6.      'Wonderful movie',
7.      'one of the best films ever',
8.      'fantastic film to watch',
9.      'great movie',
10.     'Acting and direction is brilliant'
11. ]
```

Text Classification with Machine Learning

Text classification is one of the most routinely used applications of Natural Language Processing. Text classification is a process of classifying text documents in the form of tweets, messages, emails, or articles into predefined classes based on the contents of documents. Text classification has various applications. For instance, Google uses text classification techniques to automatically separate spam emails from the original emails. Similarly, various companies use text classification to find public sentiment toward their products by analyzing their tweets or Facebook posts.

In this chapter, you will study how to perform text classification using machine learning techniques. In the next chapter, you will see how to use deep learning techniques for text classification. So, let's begin without much ado.

8.1. IMDB Movies Sentimental Analysis

The first application of text classification that you are going to study in this chapter is IMDB movies sentimental analysis. The dataset will consist of public reviews on IMDB (www.imdb.com), and the task will be to classify reviews as having positive or negative opinions regarding movies. So let's start.

The first step is to import the required libraries.

8.1.1. Importing Libraries

Script 1:

```
1. import numpy as np
2. import pandas as pd
3. import re
4. import nltk
5. import matplotlib.pyplot as plt
6. import seaborn as sns
7. %matplotlib inline
```

The dataset for this task is available by the name "imdb.reviews. csv" in the *data folder in the book resources*. The following script imports the CSV file into your application and prints the first five rows of the dataset.

8.1.2. Importing the Dataset

Script 2:

```
1. data_path = "E:/Datasets/imdb_reviews.csv"
2. movie_dataset = pd.read_csv(data_path, engine='python')
3. movie_dataset.head()
```

Output:

	SentimentText	Sentiment
0	first think another Disney movie, might good, ...	1
1	Put aside Dr. House repeat missed, Desperate H...	0
2	big fan Stephen King's work, film made even gr...	1
3	watched horrid thing TV. Needless say one movi...	0
4	truly enjoyed film. acting terrific plot. Jeff...	1

From the output, you can see that the dataset contains two columns *SentimentText* and *Sentiment*. The former contains the text reviews about movies, while the latter contains user opinions for corresponding movies. In the sentiment column, 1 refers to a positive opinion, while 0 refers to a negative opinion.

Let's see the number of rows in the dataset.

Script 3:

```
movie_dataset.shape
```

The output shows that the dataset contains 25,000 records.

Output:

```
(25000, 2)
```

Next, we can print the distribution of positive and negative user reviews using a pie chart as shown below:

Script 4:

```
1. plt.rcParams["figure.figsize"] = [8,10]
2. movie_dataset.Sentiment.value_counts().plot(kind='pie',
   autopct='%1.0f%%')
```

Output:

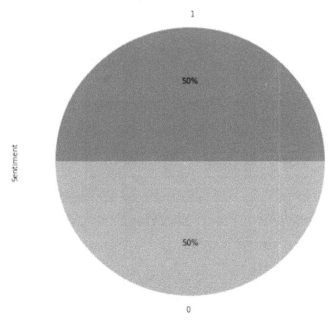

The pie chart shows that half of the reviews are positive, while the other half contains negative reviews.

8.1.3. Cleaning the Data

Before we actually train our machine learning model on the training data, we need to remove the special characters and numbers from our text. Removing special characters and numbers create empty spaces in the text, which also need to be removed.

Before cleaning the data, let's first divide the data into text reviews and user sentiment.

Script 5:

```
1. X = movie_dataset["SentimentText"]
2.
3. y = movie_dataset["Sentiment"]
```

The following script defines a **clean_text()** method, which accepts a text string and returns a string that is cleaned of digits, special characters, and multiple empty spaces. The process of text cleaning has been explained in detail in chapter 4.

Script 6:

```
1.  def clean_text(doc):
2.
3.
4.      document = re.sub('[^a-zA-Z]', ' ', doc)
5.
6.      document = re.sub(r"\s+[a-zA-Z]\s+", ' ', document)
7.
8.      document = re.sub(r'\s+', ' ', document)
9.
10.     return document
```

The following script calls the **clean_text()** method and preprocesses all the user reviews in the dataset.

Script 7:

```
1.  X_sentences = []
2.  reviews = list(X)
3.  for rev in reviews:
4.      X_sentences.append(clean_text(rev))
```

8.1.4. Convert Text to Numbers

In chapter 7, you studied that we need to convert a text document to numbers before we can apply machine learning techniques to the text document. In this regard, you studied various techniques, i.e., Bag of Words, TF-IDF, Word Embeddings, etc. In this section, you will use the TF-IDF technique for converting text to numbers. In the next chapter, you will use word embeddings.

The following script converts text to numbers. Here, the **max_features** attribute specifies that a maximum of 2,000 most occurring words should be used to create a feature dictionary. The **min_df** attribute here specifies to only include words that occur for a minimum of five times across all the documents. **Max_df** defines not to include words that occur in more than 70 percent of the documents.

Script 8:

```
1.  from nltk.corpus import stopwords
2.  from sklearn.feature_extraction.text import TfidfVectorizer
3.
4.  vectorizer = TfidfVectorizer (max_features=2000, min_df=5,
    max_df=0.7, stop_words=stopwords.words('english'))
5.  X= vectorizer.fit_transform(X_sentences).toarray()
```

The text data has been processed. Now, we can train our machine learning model on text.

8.1.5. Training the Model

We will be developing a supervised text classification model since, in the dataset, we already have the public sentiment. We will divide our data into the training and test set. The algorithm will learn the relationship between text reviews and the opinion using the training data since both text reviews and corresponding opinions are given in the training dataset.

Once the machine learning model is trained on the training data, the test data, including only the text reviews, will be given as input to the model. The model will then predict the unknown sentiment for all the text reviews.

The predicted sentiment is then compared with the actual sentiment in the test data in order to evaluate the performance of the text classification model.

The following script divides the data into training and test sets.

Script 9:

```
1.  from sklearn.model_selection import train_test_split
2.  X_train, X_test, y_train, y_test = train_test_split(X, y,
    test_size=0.20, random_state=42)
```

To train the machine learning model, you will be using the **RandomForestClassifier** (https://bit.ly/2V1GOkO) model, which is one of the most commonly used machine learning models for classification.

The **fit()** method of the **RandomForestClassifier** class is used to train the model.

Script 10:

```
1.  from sklearn.ensemble import RandomForestClassifier
2.
3.  clf = RandomForestClassifier(n_estimators=250, random_
    state=0)
4.  clf.fit(X_train, y_train)
```

8.1.6. Evaluating Model Performance

Once a supervised machine learning model is trained, you can make predictions on the test. To do so, you can use the **predict()** method of the **RandomForestClassifer**. To compare predictions with the actual output, you can use confusion matrix, accuracy, recall, and F1 measures. The following script evaluates the model performance.

Script 11:

```
1. y_pred = clf.predict(X_test)
2.
3. from sklearn.metrics import classification_report,
   confusion_matrix, accuracy_score
4.
5. print(confusion_matrix(y_test,y_pred))
6. print(classification_report(y_test,y_pred))
7. print(accuracy_score(y_test,y_pred))
```

Output:

```
[[2078  405]
 [ 420 2097]]
              precision    recall  f1-score   support

           0       0.83      0.84      0.83      2483
           1       0.84      0.83      0.84      2517

    accuracy                           0.83      5000
   macro avg       0.83      0.84      0.83      5000
weighted avg       0.84      0.83      0.84      5000

0.835
```

The output shows that our model achieves an accuracy of 83.5 percent on the test set.

8.1.7. Making Predictions on Single Instance

Now, we are ready to make predictions on a new text. The text is first converted into text form using the same TfidfVectorizer that is used to convert text to numbers for training the model. The numeric form of the text can then be passed to the *predict* method of the classifier object to make predictions. In the following script, we try to find the sentiment of a random sentence: "The movie was really good, I liked it."

Script 12:

```
print(clf.predict(vectorizer.transform(["The movie was really
good, I liked it"])))
```

Output:

```
[1]
```

The output shows a sentiment of 1, which means that our model thinks this is a positive review, which it actually is. Hence, we can say that our text classification model is doing a good job.

8.2. Ham and Spam Message Classification

In the previous section, you saw an example of text classification for the sentimental analysis of movie reviews. In this section, you will see how we can use text classification for ham and spam message classification. A ham message is an original and genuine message, whereas a spam message contains spam information such as "Nigerian princess offering you $ 10 million."

The process of ham and spam message classification is very similar to sentiment analysis.

8.2.1. Importing Libraries

We start by importing the libraries.

Script 13:

```
8.  import numpy as np
9.  import pandas as pd
10. import re
11. import nltk
12. import matplotlib.pyplot as plt
13. import seaborn as sns
14. %matplotlib inline
```

8.2.2. Importing the Dataset

The dataset for this task is available at this Github link: https://bit.ly/3djTeyX.

The dataset is also available in the *data folder of the book resources* by the name *spam.csv*.

The following script imports the dataset and displays its first five rows.

Script 14:

```
1.  data_path = "https://raw.githubusercontent.com/mohitgupta-
    omg/Kaggle-SMS-Spam-Collection-Dataset-/master/spam.csv"
2.  message_dataset = pd.read_csv(data_path, engine='python')
3.  message_dataset.head()
```

Output:

	v1	v2	Unnamed: 2	Unnamed: 3	Unnamed: 4
0	ham	Go until jurong point, crazy.. Available only ...	NaN	NaN	NaN
1	ham	Ok lar... Joking wif u oni...	NaN	NaN	NaN
2	spam	Free entry in 2 a wkly comp to win FA Cup fina...	NaN	NaN	NaN
3	ham	U dun say so early hor... U c already then say...	NaN	NaN	NaN
4	ham	Nah I don't think he goes to usf, he lives aro...	NaN	NaN	NaN

The output shows that the dataset contains five columns. However, only the columns v1 and v2 contain the data we need. The v1 column contains information about whether a message is a spam or ham, while the v2 column contains the text of a message.

The following script shows the total number of rows in the dataset:

Script 15:

```
movie_dataset.shape
```

Output:

```
(5572, 5)
```

The output shows that the dataset contains 5,572 rows.

Since we only need columns v1 and v2, we will filter these two columns and remove the remaining columns, as shown in the following script:

Script 16:

```
1. message_dataset = message_dataset.filter(["v1", "v2"])
2. message_dataset.head()
```

Output:

	v1	v2
0	ham	Go until jurong point, crazy.. Available only ...
1	ham	Ok lar... Joking wif u oni...
2	spam	Free entry in 2 a wkly comp to win FA Cup fina...
3	ham	U dun say so early hor... U c already then say...
4	ham	Nah I don't think he goes to usf, he lives aro...

The following script plots the distribution of ham and spam messages.

Script 17:

```
3. plt.rcParams["figure.figsize"] = [8,10]
4. movie_dataset.Sentiment.value_counts().plot(kind='pie',
   autopct='%1.0f%%')
```

Output:

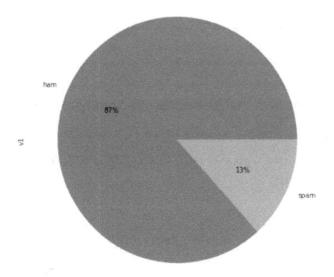

The output shows that 87 percent of the messages are ham, while only 13 percent of the messages are spam.

8.2.3. Cleaning the Data

The following script divides the data into features and labels. The feature set consists of text contents of the messages, while the labels correspond to the information about whether the messages are spam or ham.

Script 18:

```
1. X = message_dataset["v2"]
2.
3. y = message_dataset["v1"]
```

The following script defines **clean_text()** that cleans the text messages.

Script 19:

```
11. def clean_text(doc):
12.
13.
14.     document = re.sub('[^a-zA-Z]', ' ', doc)
15.
16.     document = re.sub(r"\s+[a-zA-Z]\s+", ' ', document)
17.
18.     document = re.sub(r'\s+', ' ', document)
19.
20.     return document
```

The following script cleans all the messages in the dataset.

Script 20:

```
5. X_sentences = []
6. reviews = list(X)
7. for rev in reviews:
8.     X_sentences.append(clean_text(rev))
```

8.2.4. Convert Text to Numbers

As we did for sentiment analysis, we need to convert text to numbers for ham and spam classification, as well. The following script uses the TF-IDF approach for converting text to numbers.

Script 21:

```
6. from nltk.corpus import stopwords
7. from sklearn.feature_extraction.text import TfidfVectorizer
8.
9. vectorizer = TfidfVectorizer (max_features=2000, min_df=5,
   max_df=0.7, stop_words=stopwords.words('english'))
10. X= vectorizer.fit_transform(X_sentences).toarray()
```

8.2.5. Training the Model

The data is now ready for training a machine learning model. But first, we need to divide our data into the training and test sets, which the following script does.

Script 22:

```
3.  from sklearn.model_selection import train_test_split
4.  X_train, X_test, y_train, y_test = train_test_split(X, y,
    test_size=0.20, random_state=42)
```

Finally, the model training is performed in the following script.

Script 23:

```
5.  from sklearn.ensemble import RandomForestClassifier
6.
7.  clf = RandomForestClassifier(n_estimators=250, random_
    state=0)
8.  clf.fit(X_train, y_train)
```

8.2.6. Evaluating Model Performance

The last step is to make predictions on the training set and evaluate the model performance, which is done in the following script:

Script 24:

```
8.  y_pred = clf.predict(X_test)
9.
10. from sklearn.metrics import classification_report,
    confusion_matrix, accuracy_score
11.
12. print(confusion_matrix(y_test,y_pred))
13. print(classification_report(y_test,y_pred))
14. print(accuracy_score(y_test,y_pred))
```

Output:

```
[[963    2]
 [ 20 130]]
              precision    recall  f1-score   support

         ham       0.98      1.00      0.99       965
        spam       0.98      0.87      0.92       150

    accuracy                           0.98      1115
   macro avg       0.98      0.93      0.96      1115
weighted avg       0.98      0.98      0.98      1115

0.9802690582959641
```

The output shows that the accuracy of our model is 98.02 percent while predicting whether a message is a spam or ham, which is pretty impressive.

8.2.7. Making Predictions on Single Instance

As we did for sentimental analysis, we can make predictions on a single sentence. Let's fetch a sentence randomly from our dataset.

Script 25:

```
1.  print(X_sentences[56])
2.  print(y[56])
```

Output:

```
Congrats year special cinema pass for is yours call now
Suprman Matrix StarWars etc all FREE bx ip we pm Dont miss out
spam
```

The output shows that the sentence number 56 in the dataset is spam. The text of the sentence is also shown in the output. Let's pass this sentence into our ham and spam text classifier and see what it thinks:

Script 26:

```
print(clf.predict(vectorizer.transform([X_sentences[56]])))
```

Output:

```
['spam']
```

The model correctly classified the message as spam.

Further Readings – Machine Learning and Confusion Matrix

To know more about Machine Learning Algorithms supported by Scikit Learn, check this link: https://bit.ly/2YfKG7Q.

To study more about confusion matrix, accuracy, F1, recall, and precision, check this link: https://bit.ly/3hW2JI6.

Hands-on Time – Exercise

Now, it is your turn. Follow the instructions in **the exercises below** to check your understanding of text classification with NLTK and Sklearn. The answers to these questions are given at the end of the book.

Exercise 8.1

Question 1:

Which attribute of the TfidfVectorizer vectorizer is used to define the minimum word count?

    A. min_word

    B. min_count

    C. min_df

    D. None of the Above

Question 2:

Which method of the RandomForestClassifier object is used to train the algorithm on the input data?

    A. train()

    B. fit()

    C. predict()

    D. train_data()

Question 3:

Sentimental analysis with RandomForestClassifier is a type of _____ learning problem.

    A. Supervised

    B. Unsupervised

    C. Reinforcement

    D. Lazy

Exercise 8.2

Use CountVectorizer to perform sentimental analysis of the "imdb_reviews.csv" dataset available in the *data folder of the book resources*. See if you can get better performance with CountVectorizer compared to the TfidfVectorizer.

Text Summarization and Topic Modeling

Text summarization and topic modeling are very common applications of Natural Language Processing. In this chapter, you will how to perform text summarization and topic modeling with the help of examples.

9.1. Text Summarization with NLTK

In-text summarization, as the name suggests, the task is to summarize a given piece of text. There are two main types of text summarization techniques:

1. Extractive Summaries

In extractive summary, the important piece of text from the original text is included in the summarized text. The summary basically consists of the aggregate of important parts from the original text. The wording of the original text is not changed in the summarized text.

2. Abstractive Summaries

In an abstractive summary, the original text is fully understood and then summarized in totally new words representing the gist of the original articles.

Extractive summaries are easy to perform, and hence, most of the existing NLP approaches perform extractive text summaries.

Let's see an example. Suppose you have the following piece of text, and you want to summarize it.

> Climate change is real. Glaciers are melting. With climate change world temperature is rising. Weathers have become extreme. Climate change has affected agriculture and industry equally. The seasons are changing their cycle. Measures are needed to control this phenomenon.

You can do so with an extractive summary approach. The approach that we are going to use is simple. First, we have to divide our text into sentences, as shown in the following script.

```
1.  import nltk
2.  scrapped_data = """The climate change is real. Glaciers
    are melting.
3.  With climate change world temperature is rising. Weathers
    have become extreme.
4.  Climate change has affected agriculture and industry
    equally.
5.  The seasons are changing their cycle. Measures are needed
    to control this phenomenon."""
6.
7.  all_sentences = nltk.sent_tokenize(scrapped_data)
```

Next, we have to assign a frequency of occurrence to all the words in all the sentences of the input text.

```
1.  stopwords = nltk.corpus.stopwords.words('english')
2.
3.  word_freq = {}
4.  for word in nltk.word_tokenize(scrapped_data):
5.      if word not in stopwords:
6.          if word not in word_freq.keys():
7.              word_freq[word] = 1
8.          else:
9.              word_freq[word] += 1
```

Let's see the frequency of all the words in our text document:

```
print(word_freq)
```

Output:

```
{'The': 2, 'climate': 2, 'change': 3, 'real': 1, '.':
7, 'Glaciers': 1, 'melting': 1, 'With': 1, 'world': 1,
'temperature': 1, 'rising': 1, 'Weathers': 1, 'become': 1,
'extreme': 1, 'Climate': 1, 'affected': 1, 'agriculture':
1, 'industry': 1, 'equally': 1, 'season': 1, 'changing':
1, 'cycle': 1, 'Measures': 1, 'needed': 1, 'control': 1,
'phenomenon': 1}
```

You can see that the word climate occurs twice, change occurs three times, and so on. Next, we need to find the relative frequency of each word. The relative frequency for a word can be calculated by dividing the frequency of a word by the frequency of the most occurring word. The following script does that.

```
1.  max_freq = max(word_freq.values())
2.
3.  for word in word_freq.keys():
4.      word_freq[word] = (word_freq[word]/max_freq)
```

Let's print the relative frequencies.

```
print(word_freq)
```

Output:

```
{'The': 0.2857142857142857, 'climate': 0.2857142857142857,
'change': 0.42857142857142855, 'real': 0.14285714285714285,
'.': 1.0, 'Glaciers': 0.14285714285714285, 'melting':
0.14285714285714285, 'With': 0.14285714285714285, 'world':
0.14285714285714285, 'temperature': 0.14285714285714285,
'rising': 0.14285714285714285, 'Weathers':
0.14285714285714285, 'become': 0.14285714285714285, 'extreme':
0.14285714285714285, 'Climate': 0.14285714285714285,
'affected': 0.14285714285714285, 'agriculture':
0.14285714285714285, 'industry': 0.14285714285714285,
'equally': 0.14285714285714285, 'season': 0.14285714285714285,
'changing': 0.14285714285714285, 'cycle': 0.14285714285714285,
'Measures': 0.14285714285714285, 'needed':
0.14285714285714285, 'control': 0.14285714285714285,
'phenomenon': 0.14285714285714285}
```

The last step is to calculate the frequency scores of all the sentences in the corpus. The frequency score for a sentence is equal to the sum of the frequency scores for all the words in the sentence. The following script calculates frequency scores for all the sentences in the corpus.

```
1.  sentence_scores = {}
2.  for sentence in all_sentences:
3.      for token in nltk.word_tokenize(sentence.lower()):
4.          if token in word_freq.keys():
5.              if len(sentence.split(' ')) <25:
6.                  if sentence not in sentence_scores.keys():
7.                      sentence_scores[sentence] = word_
    freq[token]
8.                  else:
9.                      sentence_scores[sentence] += word_
    freq[token]
```

```
print(sentence_scores)
```

The following output shows the frequency scores for all the sentences.

Output:

```
{'The climate change is real.': 1.857142857142857, 'Glaciers
are melting.': 1.1428571428571428, 'With climate change
world temperature is rising.': 2.1428571428571423, 'Weathers
have become extreme.': 1.2857142857142856, 'Climate
change has affected agriculture and industry equally.':
2.2857142857142856, 'The season are changing their cycle.':
1.4285714285714286, 'Measures are needed to control this
phenomenon.': 1.4285714285714286}
```

To summarize, select the N sentences with the highest frequencies. For instance, the following script selects the top three sentences with the highest frequencies.

```
1. import heapq
2. selected_sentences= heapq.nlargest(3, sentence_scores,
   key=sentence_scores.get)
3.
4. text_summary = ' '.join(selected_sentences)
5. print(text_summary)
```

Here is the output.

Output:

```
Climate change has affected agriculture and industry equally.
With climate change world temperature is rising. Climate
change is real.
```

The summary looks quite meaningful. This is just a very crude example. In the next section, you will see how we can summarize a Wikipedia article.

First, you need to install the beautifulsoup4 and lxml libraries. You need these libraries to scrape the Wikipedia article that we are going to summarize. Execute the following commands on your command terminal to install these libraries.

```
$ pip install beautifulsoup4
$ pip install lxml
```

9.1.1. Scraping Wikipedia Article

The following script scrapes the Wikipedia article on natural language processing. The script parses the article, and then creates a corpus that contains text from all the paragraphs in the article, ignoring the HTML tags.

Script 1:

```
1.  import bs4 as bs
2.  import urllib.request
3.  import re
4.
5.  raw_data = urllib.request.urlopen('https://en.wikipedia.
    org/wiki/Natural_language_processing')
6.  document = raw_data.read()
7.
8.  parsed_document = bs.BeautifulSoup(document,'lxml')
9.
10. article_paras = parsed_document.find_all('p')
11.
12. scrapped_data = ""
13.
14. for para in article_paras:
15.     scrapped_data += para.text
```

The first 1,000 characters of the scraped text look like this.

Script 2:

```
print(scrapped_data[:1000])
```

Output:

```
Natural language processing (NLP) is a subfield of linguistics,
computer science, information engineering, and artificial
intelligence concerned with the interactions between computers
and human (natural) languages, in particular how to program
computers to process and analyze large amounts of natural
language data.
```

> Challenges in natural language processing frequently involve speech recognition, natural language understanding, and natural language generation.
>
> The history of natural language processing (NLP) generally started in the 1950s, although work can be found from earlier periods.
>
> In 1950, Alan Turing published an article titled "Computing Machinery and Intelligence," which proposed what is now called the Turing test as a criterion of intelligence[clarification needed].
>
> The Georgetown experiment in 1954 involved fully automatic translation of more than sixty Russian sentences into English. The authors claimed that within three or five years, machine translation would be a solved p

9.1.2. Text Cleaning

The next step is to clean the text of digits and special characters.

Script 3:

```
1. scrapped_data = re.sub(r'\[[0-9]*\]', ' ', scrapped_data)
2. scrapped_data = re.sub(r'\s+', ' ', scrapped_data)
3.
4. formatted_text = re.sub('[^a-zA-Z]', ' ', scrapped_data)
5. formatted_text = re.sub(r'\s+', ' ', formatted_text)
```

9.1.3. Finding Word Frequencies

The rest of the process is similar. You have to first divide the text into sentences.

Script 4:

```
1. import nltk
2. all_sentences = nltk.sent_tokenize(scrapped_data)
```

Next, from the cleaned data, you create a word frequency dictionary that contains words and their corresponding frequency of occurrence.

Script 5:

```
1.  stopwords = nltk.corpus.stopwords.words('english')
2.
3.  word_freq = {}
4.  for word in nltk.word_tokenize(formatted_text):
5.      if word not in stopwords:
6.          if word not in word_freq.keys():
7.              word_freq[word] = 1
8.          else:
9.              word_freq[word] += 1
```

The next step is to create relative frequencies of the words as shown below:

Script 6:

```
1.  max_freq = max(word_freq.values())
2.
3.  for word in word_freq.keys():
4.      word_freq[word] = (word_freq[word]/max_freq)
```

9.1.4. Finding Sentence Scores

Finally, the frequency scores for sentences can be calculated by adding the frequency scores of all the words in a sentence, which is achieved in the following script. Remember, very long sentences are ignored, and only sentences containing less than 25 words are included in the summary. You can increase or decrease this number.

Script 7:

```
1.  sentence_scores = {}
2.  for sentence in all_sentences:
3.      for token in nltk.word_tokenize(sentence.lower()):
4.          if token in word_freq.keys():
5.              if len(sentence.split(' ')) <25:
6.                  if sentence not in sentence_scores.keys():
7.                      sentence_scores[sentence] = word_
    freq[token]
8.                  else:
9.                      sentence_scores[sentence] += word_
    freq[token]
```

9.1.5. Printing Summaries

The last step is to select the top N sentences in the ascending order of the frequency scores. The following script selects the top five sentences.

Script 8:

```
1.  import heapq
2.  selected_sentences= heapq.nlargest(5, sentence_scores,
    key=sentence_scores.get)
3.
4.  text_summary = ' '.join(selected_sentences)
5.  print(text_summary)
```

Output:

```
Challenges in natural language processing frequently involve
speech recognition, natural language understanding, and
natural language generation. Starting in the late 1980s,
however, there was a revolution in natural language processing
with the introduction of machine learning algorithms for
language processing. Since the so-called "statistical
revolution" in the late 1980s and mid-1990s, much natural
language processing research has relied heavily on machine
learning. Little further research in machine translation was
conducted until the late 1980s when the first statistical
machine translation systems were developed. Up to the 1980s,
most natural language processing systems were based on complex
sets of hand-written rules.
```

The output shows the summary of the Wikipedia article on Natural Language Processing.

9.2. Topic Modeling with LDA Using Gensim

Topic modeling is a common NLP task, which attempts to find the topics within a text document. Notice that topic modeling is an unsupervised approach, and topic modeling only gives you an idea of which words frequently occur. It is then up to you to deduce the topic having seen the frequently and co-occurring words.

We will be using the Gensim library to perform topic modeling. Also, to scrape Wikipedia articles, we will be using the Python Wikipedia module.

Execute the following commands on your command terminal to install the Wikipedia and Gensim libraries.

```
$ pip install wikipedia
$ pip install gensim
```

9.2.1. Wikipedia Article Scraping

We will scrape four articles from Wikipedia. The article topics are Machine Learning, Pizza, Coronavirus, and Eiffel Tower. The articles are scraped, and then the content of the articles is retrieved via the "content" property of the "page" object.

Script 9:

```python
1.  import wikipedia
2.  import nltk
3.  import re
4.  from nltk.stem import WordNetLemmatizer
5.
6.  stemmer = WordNetLemmatizer()
7.
8.  nltk.download('stopwords')
9.  en_stop = set(nltk.corpus.stopwords.words('english'))
10.
11. ml = wikipedia.page("Machine Learning")
12. pizza = wikipedia.page("Pizza")
13. covid = wikipedia.page("Corona Virus")
14. etower = wikipedia.page("Eiffel Tower")
15.
16. corpus = [ml.content, pizza.content, covid.content,
    etower.content]
```

9.2.2. Data Cleaning

The next step is to clean all the data, convert the data into tokens, convert the tokens to lower case, remove stop words, lemmatize the tokens, and remove all the tokens smaller in size than five characters. Tokens here refer to words. The **clean_text()** method performs all these tasks.

Script 10:

```
1. def clean_text(doc):
2.
3.     doc = re.sub(r'\W', ' ', str(doc))
4.
5.     doc = re.sub(r'\s+[a-zA-Z]\s+', ' ', str(doc))
6.
7.     doc = re.sub(r"\s+[a-zA-Z]\s+", ' ', doc)
8.
9.     doc = re.sub(r'\s+', ' ', doc)
10.
11.     doc = re.sub(r'^b\s+', '', doc)
12.
13.     doc = doc.lower()
14.
15.     words = doc.split()
16.     words = [stemmer.lemmatize(word) for word in words]
17.     words = [word for word in words if word not in en_
    stop]
18.     words = [word for word in words if len(word) > 5]
19.
20.     return words
```

The following script converts the data into a cleaned and preprocessed collection of words by passing the data into **clean_text()** method.

Script 11:

```
1. formated_data = [];
2. for doc in corpus:
3.     words = clean_text(doc)
4.     formated_data.append(words)
```

9.2.3. Topic Modeling with LDA

LDA (Latent Dirichlet Allocation) is one of the most commonly used algorithms for topic modeling. The LDA model makes two assumptions:

1. Text documents that contain similar words have the same topic.

2. Text documents containing a group of words that frequently occur together have the same topic.

The Gensim library contains an implementation of the LDA model. However, before you can use that, you need to create a Gensim corpus containing all the words in the input text. The Gensim corpus is a BOW model created using a Genism dictionary. To create a Genism dictionary, you need to pass a collection of formatted words to the Dictionary object of the Corpora module from the Gensim library. To create a Gensim corpus, you need to pass the Gensim dictionary to the **doc2bow()** method of the Gensim dictionary, the dictionary returns Gensim corpus as shown in the following script.

Script 12:

```
1.  from gensim import corpora
2.
3.  gensim_dict = corpora.Dictionary(formated_data)
4.  gensim_corpus = [gensim_dict.doc2bow(word, allow_
    update=True) for word in formated_data]
```

To create an LDA model with Gensim, you can use the **LdaModel** class from the **gensim.models.ldamodel module**. The number of topics that you want to extract is passed to the **num_topics** attribute, while the Gensim corpus is passed as the first attribute. The **passes** attribute refers to the number of iterations that you want to use to train your LDA model. Look at the following script:

Script 13:

```
1. import gensim
2.
3. lda_topic_models = gensim.models.ldamodel.LdaModel(gensim_
   corpus, num_topics=4, id2word=gensim_dict, passes=20)
```

Once the model is trained, you can extract N number of words per topic. The following script extracts seven words per topic, i.e., 28 words in total.

Script 14:

```
1. lda_topics = lda_topic_models.print_topics(num_words=7)
2. for topic_name in lda_topics:
3.     print(topic_name)
```

Output:

```
(0, '0.029*"eiffel" + 0.009*"second" + 0.006*"structure" +
    0.006*"french" + 0.006*"exposition" + 0.006*"tallest" +
    0.005*"engineer"')
(1, '0.000*"learning" + 0.000*"coronavirus" + 0.000*"machine"
    + 0.000*"algorithm" + 0.000*"coronaviruses" +
    0.000*"eiffel" + 0.000*"training"')

(2, '0.013*"cheese" + 0.009*"italian" + 0.009*"tomato" +
    0.007*"ingredient" + 0.007*"similar" + 0.007*"topped" +
    0.007*"topping"')

(3, '0.038*"learning" + 0.021*"machine" + 0.021*"coronavirus"
    + 0.013*"algorithm" + 0.010*"training" +
    0.009*"coronaviruses" + 0.007*"example"')
```

The output shows that the words from the first topic, e.g., Eiffel, engineer, tallest, structure, French, etc., refer to some tall building in France. Since the word Eiffel is explicitly there, we can say that one of the topics in our text is related to the Eiffel Tower.

The words that belong to the second topic are learning, machine, and algorithm. Hence, we can conclude that the second topic is related to machine learning. In the same way, it can be concluded that the third topic is related to pizza, while the last topic is related to coronavirus.

You can see that though in some cases, one topic contains mixed words such as in topic 4, we have machine learning, coronavirus which can be considered noise since our topic model is not 100 percent correct.

9.2.4. Testing the Topic Model

The last step is to test the topic model. Let's pass a sentence to our topic model, and see what topic is assigned to our sentence.

Script 15:

```
1. doc = 'I like to eat fast food filled with bread and cream'
2. formatted_doc = clean_text(doc)
3. bow_doc = gensim_dict.doc2bow(formatted_doc)
4.
5. print(lda_topic_models.get_document_topics(bow_doc))
```

Output:

```
[(0, 0.1330796), (1, 0.12547417), (2, 0.6163538), (3,
    0.12509239)]
```

The output shows that there is a 13.30 percent probability that our sentence belongs to topic 1, 12.54 percent probability that it belongs to topic 2, 61.63 percent probability that it belongs to topic 3, while 12.50 percent probability that it belongs to topic 4. So, the highest probability is that our sentence belongs to topic 3, which is Pizza. We actually talk about food in our sentence. Hence, we can say that our topic model has made a correct prediction.

Further Readings – Topic Modeling

To know more about topic modeling, look at this article:

https://bit.ly/3hFhuyG

Hands-on Time – Exercise

Now, it is your turn. Follow the instructions in **the exercises below** to check your understanding of word text summarization and topic modeling. The answers to these questions are given at the end of the book.

Exercise 9.1

Question 1:

The type of text summary that includes contents from the original text is called:

    A. Abstractive Summary

    B. Extractive Summary

    C. Derived Summary

    D. None of the Above

Question 2:

To parse a Wikipedia page, which of the following attribute of the `page` object is used?

    A. text

    B. data

    C. content

    D. raw_data

Question 3:

To create Gensim corpora, you need to pass a collection of tokens to which object:

    A. gensim.Corpora()

    B. gensim.Corpus()

    C. gensim.Collection()

    D. gensim.Dictionary()

Exercise 9.2

Using Wikipedia Library for Python, perform text summarization of the Wikipedia article on Coronavirus. Add only sentences that contain less than 40 words. Display the first 10 sentences from the summary.

10

Text Classification with Deep Learning

In chapter 8, you saw how to perform text classification using traditional machine learning techniques. You developed a movie sentiment classifier and a ham and spam message detection system using the Random Forest System. While machine learning approaches are still commonly used for text classification, deep learning approaches are gradually replacing them. With deep learning algorithms like LSTM and 1-D CNN, it is now easier to develop more complex text classification. Furthermore, Word2Vec embedding techniques can be used to represent text in way reduced dimensions. Word2Vec can be used with deep learning techniques.

In this chapter, you will see how to perform sentimental analysis, which is an application of text classification, using LSTM and 1-D CNN. So let's begin without any ado.

10.1. Sentimental Analysis with LSTM

In this section, we will be performing the text sentimental analysis of public tweets regarding different US airlines using the LSTM algorithm.

The source code for this section is run using Google colab therefore in the script for this section, you will see the code to import data from your google drive.

The dataset that we are going to use for this section is freely available at this link:

https://raw.githubusercontent.com/kolaveridi/kaggle-Twitter-US-Airline-Sentiment-/master/Tweets.csv

In addition, the data is also available in the data folder that accompanies this book.

So, let's begin without any ado. We start by importing the required libraries.

Script 1:

```
1.  import pandas as pd
2.  import numpy as np
3.  import re
4.  import nltk
5.  from nltk.corpus import stopwords
6.
7.  from numpy import array
8.  from tensorflow.keras.preprocessing.text import one_hot
9.  from tensorflow.keras.preprocessing.sequence import pad_
    sequences
10. from tensorflow.keras.models import Sequential
11. from tensorflow.keras.layers import Activation, LSTM,
    Dropout, Dense, Flatten, Input,  Embedding, Conv1D, Input
12. from tensorflow.keras.models import Model
13. from sklearn.model_selection import train_test_split
14. from tensorflow.keras.preprocessing.text import Tokenizer
```

The following script imports the dataset and displays a part of dataset header:

Script 2:

```
1. airline_data = pd.read_csv("/gdrive/My Drive/datasets/
   airline_review.csv")
2. airline_data.head()
```

Output:

airline_sentiment	airline_sentiment_confidence	negativereason	negativereason_confidence	airline	airline_sentiment_gold	name	negativereason_gold	retweet_count	text
neutral	1.0000	NaN	NaN	Virgin America	NaN	cairdin	NaN	0	@VirginAmerica What @dhepburn said
positive	0.3486	NaN	0.0000	Virgin America	NaN	jnardino	NaN	0	@VirginAmerica plus you've added commercials t...
neutral	0.6837	NaN	NaN	Virgin America	NaN	yvonnalynn	NaN	0	@VirginAmerica I didn't today... Must mean I n...
negative	1.0000	Bad Flight	0.7033	Virgin America	NaN	jnardino	NaN	0	@VirginAmerica It's really aggressive to blast...
negative	1.0000	Can't Tell	1.0000	Virgin America	NaN	jnardino	NaN	0	@VirginAmerica and it's a really big bad thing...

The airline_sentiment column contains the sentiment of tweets, and the text column contains the texts of tweets. Let's see the number of positive, negative, and neutral tweets.

Script 3:

```
airline_data.airline_sentiment.value_counts()
```

Output:

```
negative    9178
neutral     3099
positive    2363
Name: airline_sentiment, dtype: int64
```

The output shows that the majority of tweets are negative. Let's divide the data into feature and label set.

Script 4:

```
1. X = airline_data["text"]
2.
3. y = pd.get_dummies(airline_data.airline_sentiment,
   prefix='sent').values
```

Let's see the shape of the outputs.

Script 5:

```
y.shape
```

Output:

```
(14640, 3)
```

Since there are three possible labels, the output contains three columns. Let's define a function that cleans the text.

Script 6:

```
1.  def clean_text(doc):
2.
3.      document = remove_tags(doc)
4.
5.      document = re.sub('[^a-zA-Z]', ' ', document)
6.
7.      document = re.sub(r"\s+[a-zA-Z]\s+", ' ', document)
8.
9.      document = re.sub(r'\s+', ' ', document)
10.
11.     return document
```

If you have text that contains HTML contents, you can use the following function to remove HTML tags from text.

Script 7:

```
1.  TAG_RE = re.compile(r'<[^>]+>')
2.
3.  def remove_tags(document):
4.      return TAG_RE.sub('', document)
```

Next, we define a loop that cleans all the tweets.

Script 8:

```
1.  X_sentences = []
2.  reviews = list(X)
3.  for rev in reviews:
4.      X_sentences.append(clean_text(rev))
```

Finally, we divide our dataset into the training set and test set.

Script 9:

```
X_train, X_test, y_train, y_test = train_test_split(X_
sentences, y, test_size=0.20, random_state=42)
```

The next step is to convert text integers. This is done in the following script.

Script 10:

```
1.  tokenizer = Tokenizer(num_words=5000)
2.  tokenizer.fit_on_texts(X_train)
3.
4.  X_train = tokenizer.texts_to_sequences(X_train)
5.  X_test = tokenizer.texts_to_sequences(X_test)
```

Different sentences can have different lengths. Neural networks in Keras expect input sentences to be of the same length. What we can do here is find the length of the longest sentence and then add zeros to the right of the sentences that are shorter than the longest sentence. This process is called padding.

The following script performs post padding of the tweets that are smaller than 100 characters, i.e., the maximum sentence length.

Script 11:

```
1.  vocab_size = len(tokenizer.word_index) + 1
2.
3.  maxlen = 100
4.
5.  X_train = pad_sequences(X_train, padding='post',
    maxlen=maxlen)
6.  X_test = pad_sequences(X_test, padding='post',
    maxlen=maxlen)
```

Next, we have to convert numbers into word embeddings. Word embeddings, particularly the Word2Vec approach that we are going to use, have been explained in detail in chapter 7, section 5.

For word embeddings, you have two options. Either you can train your own word embeddings, or you can use pretrained word embeddings. In pretrained word embeddings, for each word, you have a pretrained vector representation. Glove and Stanford are the two most commonly used pretrained word embeddings. We will be using the Glove word embeddings in this chapter.

The Glove word embeddings are available at this link:

https://nlp.stanford.edu/projects/glove/

The link contains word embeddings of various sizes. We will be using 100-dimensional word embeddings. The word embedding file is also available in the datasets folder. The following script imports the Glove word embeddings into your application.

Script 12:

```
1.  from numpy import array
2.  from numpy import asarray
3.  from numpy import zeros
4.
5.  embedd_dict= dict()
6.  glove_embeddings = open('/gdrive/My Drive/datasets/
    glove.6B.100d.txt', encoding="utf8")
```

Next, we will create a dictionary where the keys will be the names of the words, and the values will be the corresponding word embedding vectors.

Script 13:

```
1.  for embeddings in glove_embeddings:
2.      embedding_tokens = embeddings.split()
3.      emb_word = embedding_tokens [0]
4.      emb_vector = asarray(   embedding_tokens[1:],
    dtype='float32')
5.      embedd_dict [emb_word] = emb_vector
6.
7.  glove_embeddings.close()
```

Finally, we will create a matrix where the row numbers of the matrix correspond to the index numbers for all the unique words in our dataset, and the columns contain the corresponding word embedding matrix from the Glove word embedding.

Script 14:

```
1.  embedd_mat= zeros((vocab_size, 100))
2.  for word, index in tokenizer.word_index.items():
3.      embedding_vector = embedd_dict.get(word)
4.      if embedding_vector is not None:
5.          embedd_mat[index] = embedding_vector
```

The shape of the embedding matrix is as follows.

Script 15:

```
embedd_mat.shape
```

Output:

```
(12085, 100)
```

Our embedding matrix contains 12,085 words, and one word is represented by a 100-dimensional vector.

We have created our embedding matrix that contains Glove word embeddings for the words in our corpus. Now, we can train our Neural Network Model in Keras. If you want to use word embeddings with your neural network model, you have to use **Embedding()** layer after the input layer and before any other layer in the neural network.

The first parameter to the embedding layer is your vocabulary size. The second parameter is the number of dimensions of the output vector. Also, the embedding matrix is passed to the **weights** parameter. Finally, you have to set the **trainable** attribute to **False**.

The shape of the input layer will be the maximum sentence length. If you want to connect the output of the **Embedding** layer directly to a **Dense** layer, you have to flatten the result of the Embedding layer.

The following script creates our LSTM network. The model contains two LSTM layers with 512 neurons, followed by three dense layers of 512, 256, and 3 neurons. Since there can be three possible options for sentiment in our case, i.e., positive, negative, and neutral, the final dense layer contains three neurons.

The **Softmax** function is used in the final layer since this a multiclass classification problem. Finally, **categorical cross entropy** is used as a loss function, whereas the **Adam** optimizer is used to minimize the loss.

Script 16:

```
1.  embedding_inputs = Input(shape=(maxlen))
2.  embedding_layer = Embedding(vocab_size, 100,
    weights=[embedd_mat], trainable=False)(embedding_inputs)
3.  lstm1 = LSTM(512, activation='relu', return_
    sequences=True)(embedding_layer)
4.
5.  lstm2 = LSTM(512, activation='relu',)(lstm1)
6.
7.  dense1 = Dense(512, activation='relu')(lstm2)
8.
9.  dense2 = Dense(256, activation='relu')(dense1)
10.
11. output_layer = Dense(y_train.shape[1],
    activation='softmax')(dense1)
12. model = Model(embedding_inputs, output_layer)
13.
14. model.compile(optimizer='adam', loss='categorical_
    crossentropy', metrics=['accuracy'])
```

To view the model architecture, run the following script.

Script 17:

```
1.  from tensorflow.keras.utils import plot_model
2.  plot_model(model, to_file='model_plot1.png', show_
    shapes=True, show_layer_names=True)
```

Output:

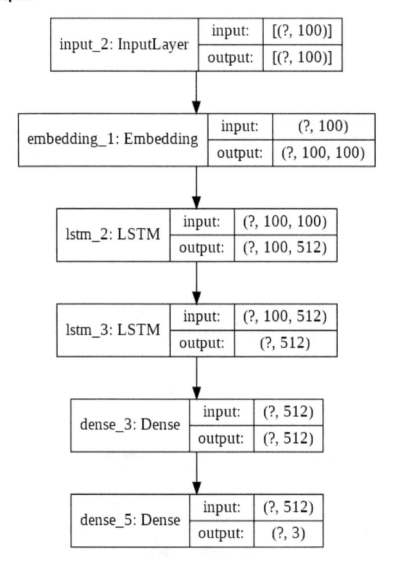

Finally, execute the following script to train the model.

Script 18:

```
1. history = model.fit(X_train, y_train, batch_size= 64,
   epochs=10, verbose=1, validation_split=0.2)
2.
3. score = model.evaluate(X_test, y_test, verbose=1)
```

Output:

```
Epoch 1/10
147/147 [==============================] - 42s 287ms/step
- loss: 1611341.2500 - accuracy: 0.6213 - val_loss: 0.9393 -
val_accuracy: 0.6265
Epoch 2/10
147/147 [==============================] - 41s 279ms/step -
loss: 500830112.0000 - accuracy: 0.6213 - val_loss: 0.9444 -
val_accuracy: 0.6265
Epoch 3/10
147/147 [==============================] - 41s 279ms/step -
loss: 1845270272.0000 - accuracy: 0.6203 - val_loss: 0.9221 -
val_accuracy: 0.6265
Epoch 4/10
147/147 [==============================] - 40s 275ms/step
- loss: 2.3222 - accuracy: 0.6213 - val_loss: 0.9172 - val_
accuracy: 0.6265
Epoch 5/10
147/147 [==============================] - 40s 275ms/step
- loss: 0.9223 - accuracy: 0.6213 - val_loss: 0.9171 - val_
accuracy: 0.6265
Epoch 6/10
147/147 [==============================] - 40s 274ms/step
- loss: 0.9222 - accuracy: 0.6213 - val_loss: 0.9169 - val_
accuracy: 0.6265
Epoch 7/10
147/147 [==============================] - 40s 274ms/step
- loss: 0.9223 - accuracy: 0.6213 - val_loss: 0.9170 - val_
accuracy: 0.6265
Epoch 8/10
147/147 [==============================] - 41s 277ms/step
- loss: 0.9222 - accuracy: 0.6213 - val_loss: 0.9170 - val_
accuracy: 0.6265
Epoch 9/10
147/147 [==============================] - 40s 272ms/step
- loss: 0.9222 - accuracy: 0.6213 - val_loss: 0.9171 - val_
accuracy: 0.6265
Epoch 10/10
```

```
147/147 [==============================] - 41s 276ms/step
- loss: 0.9222 - accuracy: 0.6213 - val_loss: 0.9169 - val_
accuracy: 0.6265
92/92 [==============================] - 3s 35ms/step - loss:
0.8951 - accuracy: 0.6452
```

At the end of the 10th epoch, we achieve an accuracy of 65.52 percent on the training set.

The following script prints the loss and accuracy on the test set.

Script 19:

```
1.  print(score[0])
2.  print(score[1])
```

Output:

```
1.084073543548584
0.7407786846160889
```

10.2. Sentiment Analysis with CNN

In this section, we will use a convolutional neural network to perform sentimental analysis of the IMDB movie reviews. The dataset for this section is available by the name "IMDB Dataset.csv" in the Dataset folder that comes with this book.

As always, you import the required libraries first.

Script 20:

```
1.  import pandas as pd
2.  import numpy as np
3.  import re
4.  import nltk
5.  from nltk.corpus import stopwords
6.
7.  from numpy import array
8.  from tensorflow.keras.preprocessing.text import one_hot
9.  from tensorflow.keras.preprocessing.sequence import pad_
    sequences
10. from tensorflow.keras.models import Sequential
11. from tensorflow.keras.layers import Activation, LSTM,
    Dropout, Dense, Flatten, Input,  Embedding, Conv1D, Input
12. from tensorflow.keras.models import Model
13. from sklearn.model_selection import train_test_split
14. from tensorflow.keras.preprocessing.text import Tokenizer
```

The following script imports the dataset.

Script 21:

```
1.    imdb_data= pd.read_csv("/gdrive/My Drive/datasets/IMDB
Dataset.csv")
2.
3.    imdb_data.head()
```

Output:

	review	sentiment
0	One of the other reviewers has mentioned that ...	positive
1	A wonderful little production. The...	positive
2	I thought this was a wonderful way to spend ti...	positive
3	Basically there's a family where a little boy ...	negative
4	Petter Mattei's "Love in the Time of Money" is...	positive

The review column contains the text review, while the sentiment column contains the sentiment of the review. Let's see how many unique sentiments we have in our dataset.

Script 22:

```
imdb_data.sentiment.value_counts()
```

Output:

```
positive     25000
negative     25000
Name: sentiment, dtype: int64
```

The output shows that we have 25,000 positive and 25,000 negative reviews in our dataset.

The following script divides the data into features and label set.

Script 23:

```
1.  X = imdb_data["review"]
2.
3.  y = pd.get_dummies(imdb_data.sentiment, prefix='sent',
    drop_first=True).values
```

Next, we define **clean_text()** function, which cleans our text reviews from punctuations and special characters.

Script 24:

```
1.  def clean_text(doc):
2.
3.      document = remove_tags(doc)
4.
5.      document = re.sub('[^a-zA-Z]', ' ', document)
6.
7.      document = re.sub(r"\s+[a-zA-Z]\s+", ' ', document)
8.
9.      document = re.sub(r'\s+', ' ', document)
10.
11.     return document
```

If you have text that contains HTML contents, you can use the following function to remove HTML tags from text.

Script 25:

```
1.  TAG_RE = re.compile(r'<[^>]+>')
2.      n
3.  def remove_tags(document):
4.      return TAG_RE.sub('', document)
```

Next, we define a loop that cleans all the tweets.

Script 26:

```
1.  X_sentences = []
2.  reviews = list(X)
3.  for rev in reviews:
4.      X_sentences.append(clean_text(rev))
```

Finally, we divide our dataset into the training set and test set.

Script 27:

```
X_train, X_test, y_train, y_test = train_test_split(X_
sentences, y, test_size=0.20, random_state=42)
```

From here on, the script will be similar to section7.2. We will perform word embedding on our text reviews.

The following script tokenizes the text and then converts text to integers.

Script 28:

```
1.  tokenizer = Tokenizer(num_words=5000)
2.  tokenizer.fit_on_texts(X_train)
3.
4.  X_train = tokenizer.texts_to_sequences(X_train)
5.  X_test = tokenizer.texts_to_sequences(X_test)
```

The following script performs post padding of the reviews that are smaller than 100 characters, i.e., the maximum sentence length.

Script 29:

```
1. vocab_size = len(tokenizer.word_index) + 1
2.
3. maxlen = 100
4.
5. X_train = pad_sequences(X_train, padding='post',
   maxlen=maxlen)
6. X_test = pad_sequences(X_test, padding='post',
   maxlen=maxlen)
```

Next, we need to import the Glove word embeddings.

Script 30:

```
1. from numpy import array
2. from numpy import asarray
3. from numpy import zeros
4.
5. embedd_dict= dict()
6. glove_embeddings = open('/gdrive/My Drive/datasets/
   glove.6B.100d.txt', encoding="utf8")
```

The following script creates the word embedding dictionary.

Script 31:

```
1. for embeddings in glove_embeddings:
2.     embedding_tokens = embeddings.split()
3.     emb_word = embedding_tokens [0]
4.     emb_vector = asarray(   embedding_tokens[1:],
   dtype='float32')
5.     embedd_dict [emb_word] = emb_vector
6.
7. glove_embeddings.close()
```

To create the embedding matrix, you can execute the following script.

Script 32:

```
1. embedd_mat= zeros((vocab_size, 100))
2. for word, index in tokenizer.word_index.items():
3.     embedding_vector = embedd_dict.get(word)
4.     if embedding_vector is not None:
5.         embedd_mat[index] = embedding_vector
```

Finally, the following script creates a CNN model for sentiment classification. The model has an input layer, an embedding layer, two convolutional layers, one flat layer, and two dense layers. Also, a dropout layer has been added after flatten and dense layers to avoid overfitting.

Script 33:

```
1. embedding_inputs = Input(shape=(maxlen))
2. embedding_layer = Embedding(vocab_size, 100,
   weights=[embedd_mat], trainable=False)(embedding_inputs)
3. conv1 = Conv1D(128, 3, strides = 2, activation= 'relu')
   (embedding_layer)
4. conv2 = Conv1D(64, 3, strides = 2, activation= 'relu')
   (conv1)
5. flat1 = Flatten()(conv2)
6. drop1 = Dropout(0.2)(flat1)
7. dense1 = Dense(512, activation = 'relu')(drop1)
8. drop2 = Dropout(0.2)(dense1)
9. output_layer = Dense(1, activation= 'sigmoid')(drop2)
10.
11. model = Model(embedding_inputs, output_layer)
12.
13. model.compile(optimizer='adam', loss='binary_
    crossentropy', metrics=['accuracy'])
```

The following script prints the CNN architecture that we are using for sentiment classification.

Script 34:

```
1. from tensorflow.keras.utils import plot_model
2. plot_model(model, to_file='model_plot1.png', show_
   shapes=True, show_layer_names=True)
```

Output:

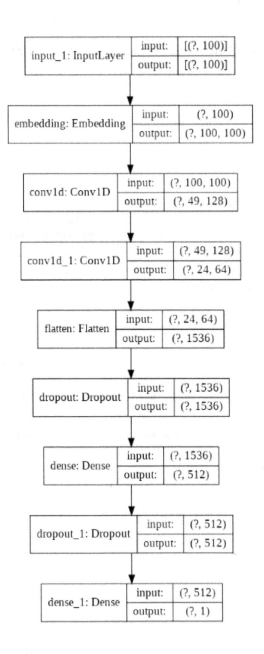

Finally, to train the model, execute the following script:

Script 35:

```
1. history = model.fit(X_train, y_train, batch_size= 64,
   epochs=10, verbose=1, validation_split=0.2)
2.
3. score = model.evaluate(X_test, y_test, verbose=1)
```

Output:

```
Epoch 1/10
500/500 [==============================] - 19s 37ms/step
- loss: 0.5289 - accuracy: 0.7250 - val_loss: 0.4257 - val_
accuracy: 0.8040
Epoch 2/10
500/500 [==============================] - 19s 37ms/step
- loss: 0.4055 - accuracy: 0.8146 - val_loss: 0.3895 - val_
accuracy: 0.8164
Epoch 3/10
500/500 [==============================] - 18s 37ms/step
- loss: 0.3660 - accuracy: 0.8346 - val_loss: 0.3856 - val_
accuracy: 0.8250
Epoch 4/10
500/500 [==============================] - 19s 38ms/step
- loss: 0.3135 - accuracy: 0.8631 - val_loss: 0.3936 - val_
accuracy: 0.8267
Epoch 5/10
500/500 [==============================] - 19s 39ms/step
- loss: 0.2682 - accuracy: 0.8841 - val_loss: 0.4436 - val_
accuracy: 0.8109
Epoch 6/10
500/500 [==============================] - 19s 39ms/step
- loss: 0.2238 - accuracy: 0.9066 - val_loss: 0.4731 - val_
accuracy: 0.8177
Epoch 7/10
500/500 [==============================] - 19s 38ms/step
- loss: 0.1810 - accuracy: 0.9257 - val_loss: 0.4826 - val_
accuracy: 0.8154
Epoch 8/10
```

```
500/500 [==============================] - 19s 38ms/step
- loss: 0.1494 - accuracy: 0.9402 - val_loss: 0.5777 - val_
accuracy: 0.7960
Epoch 9/10
500/500 [==============================] - 19s 38ms/step
- loss: 0.1180 - accuracy: 0.9534 - val_loss: 0.5960 - val_
accuracy: 0.8106
Epoch 10/10
500/500 [==============================] - 19s 38ms/step
- loss: 0.0979 - accuracy: 0.9623 - val_loss: 0.6725 - val_
accuracy: 0.8056
313/313 [==============================] - 2s 7ms/step - loss:
0.6692 - accuracy: 0.8042
```

After 10 epochs, we achieve an accuracy of 80.42 percent on the training set. To see the loss and accuracy on the test set, execute the following script:

Script 36:

```
1. print(score[0])
2. print(score[1])
```

Output:

```
0.6691895723342896
0.8041999936103821
```

On the test set, our model achieves an accuracy of 80.41 percent, which is almost similar to the training accuracy, i.e., 80.42, which shows that our model is not overfitting.

This chapter showed how to perform natural language processing via deep learning. In the next chapter, you will study autoencoder, which is an unsupervised algorithm for deep learning.

Further Readings – Text Classification with Deep Learning Using Keras

To know more about word embeddings, see these resources:
https://bit.ly/2YaCaqt

To study more about text classification with deep learning using Keras, see this link:
https://bit.ly/2YG1c17

Hands-on Time – Exercise

Now, it is your turn. Follow the instructions in **the exercises below** to check your understanding of text classification with NLTK and Sklearn. The answers to these questions are given at the end of the book.

Exercise 10.1

Question 1

Which of the following is not a pretrained word embedding?

    A. Glove

    B. Stanford

    C. Peeking

    D. All of the above

Question 2

What should be the first argument to the Keras Embedding Layer?

    A. The input vector dimensions

    B. The output vector dimensions

    C. The word embedding size

    D. The vocabulary size

Question 3

Which layer will you need to use if you want to directly connect the Embedding Layer with a Dense Layer?

    A. LSTM layer with return_sequence set to False

    B. CNN layer with max pooling

    C. Flatten layer

    D. None of the Above

Exercise 10.2

Using the ***airline_review.csv*** dataset that we used for sentiment classification in section 10.1, perform classification using a DNN (Densely Connected Neural Network).

See if you can get better results with DNN as compared to the results in section 10.1.

11

Text Translation Using Seq2Seq Model

The theory of the Seq2Seq model has been explained in section 5 of the third chapter. Seq2seq models are based on encoder-decoder architecture, which learns a mapping between input and output sentences of varying lengths. Seq2seq models can be used to develop chatbots, text translation, question-answering machines, etc.

In this chapter, you will see an application of the Seq2Seq model for text translation. So, let's begin with much ado.

11.1. Creating Seq2Seq Training Model

A Seq2seq model typically consists of two models. In the training phase, the encoder receives an input sentence and feeds it to the decoder. The decoder then predicts the output or translated sentence in our case. Both encoders and decoders are connected LSTM networks. The process is shown in the following figure. Here, the offset tag for decoder input is "<s>," and the offset tag for decoder output is </s>.

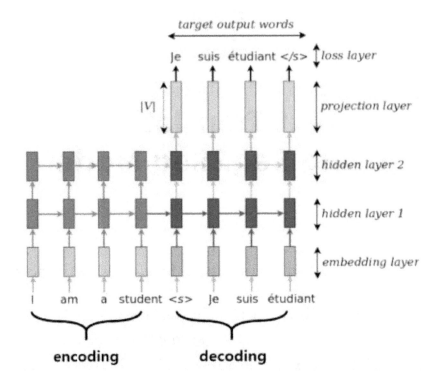

encoding   decoding

The input to the encoder is the sentence in the original language, which is English in the above example. The output of the encoder is the hidden and cell states. The input to the decoder is the hidden and cell states from the encoder plus the target dataset, one step offset.

For instance, if you look at the decoder input, in the first step, the input is always <s>. The decoder output at the first timestep is the ground truth translated output word. For instance, the first output word is "Je" in the above example. In the second step, the input to the decoder is the hidden and cell states from the previous step plus the first actual word in the output sentence, i.e., "Je." This process where the ground truth value of the previous output is fed as input to the next timestep is called Teacher Forcing. To stop the decoder from making predictions when an end of sentence tag is encountered, all the sentences are ended with an end of sentence token, which is </s> in the above diagram.

Let's code the above training model.

As always, you import the required libraries first.

Script 1:

```
1.  import os, sys
2.
3.  from keras.models import Model
4.  from keras.layers import Input, LSTM, GRU, Dense,
    Embedding
5.  from keras.preprocessing.text import Tokenizer
6.  from keras.preprocessing.sequence import pad_sequences
7.  from keras.utils import to_categorical
8.  import numpy as np
9.  import matplotlib.pyplot as plt
```

Next, we need to define a few configurations for our LSTM based encoder and decoder models as well as for the word2vec based embedding layers.

Script 2:

```
1.  BATCH_SIZE = 64
2.  NUM_EPOCHS = 20
3.  LSTM_NODES =512
4.  TOTAL_SENTENCES = 20000
5.  MAX_SEN_LENGTH = 50
6.  MAX_NUM_WORDS = 20000
7.  EMBEDDING_SIZE = 100
```

Since the script in this chapter is run using Google Collaboratory, the datasets are uploaded to Google Drive and then imported into the application. To import datasets from Google Drive to Google Collaboratory, run the following script.

Script 3:

```
1. from google.colab import drive
2. drive.mount('/gdrive')
```

The dataset that we are going to use for training our seq2seq model is available freely at this link: http://www.manythings. org/anki/.

Go to the link and then download the *fra-eng.zip* file. Unzip the file, and you should see the *fra.txt* file. This file contains our dataset. The file is also available in the *data folder in the book resources*. The first 10 lines of the file look like this:

```
1. Go.  Va !     CC-BY 2.0 (France) Attribution: tatoeba.org
   #2877272 (CM) & #1158250 (Wittydev)
2. Hi. Salut ! CC-BY 2.0 (France) Attribution: tatoeba.org
   #538123 (CM) & #509819 (Aiji)
3. Hi. Salut.  CC-BY 2.0 (France) Attribution: tatoeba.org
   #538123 (CM) & #4320462 (gillux)
4. Run!    Cours ! CC-BY 2.0 (France) Attribution: tatoeba.org
   #906328 (papabear) & #906331 (sacredceltic)
5. Run!    Courez !   CC-BY 2.0 (France) Attribution: tatoeba.
   org #906328 (papabear) & #906332 (sacredceltic)
6. Who?    Qui ?   CC-BY 2.0 (France) Attribution: tatoeba.org
   #2083030 (CK) & #4366796 (gillux)
7. Wow!    ◆a alors !  CC-BY 2.0 (France) Attribution: tatoeba.
   org #52027 (Zifre) & #374631 (zmoo)
8. Fire!   Au feu !    CC-BY 2.0 (France) Attribution: tatoeba.
   org #1829639 (Spamster) & #4627939 (sacredceltic)
9. Help!   ◆ l'aide !  CC-BY 2.0 (France) Attribution: tatoeba.
   org #435084 (lukaszpp) & #128430 (sysko)
10. Jump.   Saute.  CC-BY 2.0 (France) Attribution: tatoeba.org
    #631038 (Shishir) & #2416938 (Phoenix)
```

Each line in the *fra.txt* file contains a sentence in English, followed by a tab and then the translation of the English sentence in French, again a tab, and then the attribute.

We are only interested in the English and French sentences. The following script creates three lists. The first list contains all the English sentences, which serve as encoder input. The second list contains the decoder input sentences in French, where the offset <sos> is prefixed before all the sentences. Finally, the third list contains decoder outputs where <eos> is appended at the end of each sentence in French.

Script 4:

```
1.  input_english_sentences = []
2.  output_french_sentences = []
3.  output_french_sentences_inputs = []
4.
5.  count = 0
6.  for line in open(r'/gdrive/My Drive/datasets/fra.txt',
    encoding="utf-8"):
7.      count += 1
8.
9.      if count > TOTAL_SENTENCES:
10.         break
11.
12.     if '\t' not in line:
13.         continue
14.
15.     input_sentence = line.rstrip().split('\t')[0]
16.
17.     output = line.rstrip().split('\t')[1]
18.
19.
20.     output_sentence = output + ' <eos>'
21.     output_sentence_input = '<sos> ' + output
22.
23.     input_english_sentences.append(input_sentence)
24.     output_french_sentences.append(output_sentence)
25.     output_french_sentences_inputs.append(output_sentence_
    input)
```

Let's see how many total English and French sentences we have in our dataset:

Script 5:

```
1.  print("sentences in input:", len(input_english_sentences))
2.  print("sentences in output:", len(output_french_
    sentences))
3.  print("sentences foroutput input:", len(output_french_
    sentences_inputs))
```

Output:

```
Sentences in input: 20000
Sentences in output: 20000
Sentences for output input: 20000
```

Let's randomly print a sentence in English and its French translation (both the decoder input and the decoder output).

Script 6:

```
1.  print(input_english_sentences[175])
2.  print(output_french_sentences[175])
3.  print(output_french_sentences_inputs[175])
```

Output:

```
I'm shy.
Je suis timide. <eos>
<sos> Je suis timide.
```

You can see that the sentence at index 175 is "I'm shy." In the decoder input, the translated sentence contains <sos> tag at the beginning, while the output contains an <eos> tag.

Next, we need to tokenize both the inputs English sentences. This is a mandatory step before word embeddings.

Script 7:

```
1.  input_eng_tokenizer = Tokenizer(num_words=MAX_NUM_WORDS)
2.  input_eng_tokenizer.fit_on_texts(input_english_sentences)
3.  input_eng_integer_seq = input_eng_tokenizer.texts_to_
    sequences(input_english_sentences)
4.
5.  word2idx_eng_inputs = input_eng_tokenizer.word_index
6.  print('Sum of unique words in English sentences: %s' %
    len(word2idx_eng_inputs))
7.
8.  max_input_len = max(len(sen) for sen in input_eng_integer_
    seq)
9.  print("Length of longest sentence in English sentences:
    %g" % max_input_len)
```

Output:

```
Sum of unique words in English sentences: 3514
Length of longest sentence in English sentences: 6
```

Similarly, the following script tokenizes the output French sentences.

Script 8:

```
1.  output_french_tokenizer = Tokenizer(num_words=MAX_NUM_
    WORDS, filters='')
2.  output_french_tokenizer.fit_on_texts(output_french_
    sentences + output_french_sentences_inputs)
3.  output_french_integer_seq = output_french_tokenizer.texts_
    to_sequences(output_french_sentences)
4.  output_input_french_integer_seq = output_french_tokenizer.
    texts_to_sequences(output_french_sentences_inputs)
5.
6.  word2idx_french_outputs = output_french_tokenizer.word_
    index
7.  print('Sum of unique words in French sentences: %s' %
    len(word2idx_french_outputs))
8.
```

```
9.  num_words_output = len(word2idx_french_outputs) + 1
10. max_out_len = max(len(sen) for sen in output_french_
    integer_seq)
11. print("Length of longest sentence in French sentences: %g"
    % max_out_len)
```

Output:

```
Sum of unique words in French sentences: 9532
Length of longest sentence in French sentences: 13
```

As we did for text classification in the previous chapter, we need to pad our input and output sequences so that they can have the same length. The following script applies padding to the input sequences for the encoder.

Script 9:

```
1.  encoder_input_eng_sequences = pad_sequences(input_eng_
    integer_seq, maxlen=max_input_len)
2.  print("encoder_input_eng_sequences.shape:", encoder_input_
    eng_sequences.shape)
3.  print("encoder_input_eng_sequences[175]:", encoder_input_
    eng_sequences[175])
4.
5.  print(word2idx_eng_inputs["i'm"])
6.  print(word2idx_eng_inputs["shy"])
```

Since the maximum length of the English sentence is 6, you can see that the shape of the encoder input sentence is (20000, 6), which means that all sentences have now become of equal length of 6. For instance, if you print the padded version for the sentence at index 175, you see [0, 0, 0, 0, 6, 307]. Since the actual sentence is "I'm shy," we can print the index for these words, and see the indexes (6, 37) match indexes in the padded sequence for the sentence at index 175.

Output:

```
encoder_input_eng_sequences.shape: (20000, 6)
encoder_input_eng_sequences[175]: [  0    0    0    0    6 307]
6
307
```

Similarly, the following script applies padding to the decoder input French sentences.

Script 10:

```
1.  decoder_input_french_sequences = pad_sequences(output_
    input_french_integer_seq, maxlen=max_out_len,
    padding='post')
2.  print("decoder_input_french_sequences.shape:", decoder_
    input_french_sequences.shape)
3.  print("decoder_input_french_sequences[175]:", decoder_
    input_french_sequences[175])
4.
5.  print(word2idx_french_outputs["<sos>"])
6.  print(word2idx_french_outputs["je"])
7.  print(word2idx_french_outputs["suis"])
8.  print(word2idx_french_outputs["timide."])
```

Output:

```
decoder_input_french_sequences.shape: (20000, 13)
decoder_input_french_sequences[175]: [  2    3    6 339    0    0
0    0    0    0    0    0    0]
2
3
6
339
```

And the following script applies padding to the decoder output French sentences.

Script 11:

```
decoder_output_french_sequences = pad_sequences(output_french_
integer_seq, maxlen=max_out_len, padding='post')
```

The next step is to create word embeddings for the input and output sentences. For the input sentences, we can use the Glove word embeddings, since the sentences are English. The following script creates the embedding dictionary for the Glove word vectors.

Script 12:

```
1.  from numpy import array
2.  from numpy import asarray
3.  from numpy import zeros
4.
5.  embeddings_dictionary = dict()
6.
7.  glove_file = open(r'/gdrive/My Drive/datasets/
    glove.6B.100d.txt', encoding="utf8")
8.
9.  for line in glove_file:
10.     records = line.split()
11.     word = records[0]
12.     vector_dimensions = asarray(records[1:],
    dtype='float32')
13.     embeddings_dictionary[word] = vector_dimensions
14. glove_file.close()
```

And the following script creates an embedding matrix that will be used in the embedding layer to the encoder LSTM.

Script 13:

```
1.  num_words = min(MAX_NUM_WORDS, len(word2idx_eng_inputs) +
    1)
2.  embedding_matrix = zeros((num_words, EMBEDDING_SIZE))
3.  for word, index in word2idx_eng_inputs.items():
4.      embedding_vector = embeddings_dictionary.get(word)
5.      if embedding_vector is not None:
6.          embedding_matrix[index] = embedding_vector
```

The following script creates an embedding layer for the encoder LSTM.

Script 14:

```
embedding_layer = Embedding(num_words, EMBEDDING_SIZE,
weights=[embedding_matrix], input_length=max_input_len)
```

The next step is to create a decoder embedding layer. The first step is to create an empty embedding matrix of the shape (number of output sentence, length of longest sentence in output, and the total number of unique words in the output). The following script does that.

Script 15:

```
1.  decoder_one_hot_targets = np.zeros((
2.          len(input_english_sentences),
3.          max_out_len,
4.          num_words_output
5.      ),
6.      dtype='float32'
7.  )
```

Script 16:

```
decoder_one_hot_targets.shape
```

Output:

```
(20000, 13, 9533)
```

The next step is to add one at those indexes in the decoder embedding matrix, where a word exists in the original decoder input and output sequences.

Script 17:

```
1.  for i, d in enumerate(decoder_output_french_sequences):
2.      for t, word in enumerate(d):
3.          decoder_one_hot_targets[i, t, word] = 1
```

The following script creates the encoder model.

Script 18:

```
1. encoder_inputs_eng_placeholder = Input(shape=(max_input_
   len,))
2. x = embedding_layer(encoder_inputs_eng_placeholder)
3. encoder = LSTM(LSTM_NODES, return_state=True)
4.
5. encoder_outputs, h, c = encoder(x)
6. encoder_states = [h, c]
```

And the following script creates the decoder model. You can see that in the decoder model, a custom embedding layer is being used.

Script 19:

```
1. decoder_inputs_french_placeholder = Input(shape=(max_out_
   len,))
2.
3. decoder_embedding = Embedding(num_words_output, LSTM_
   NODES)
4. decoder_inputs_x = decoder_embedding(decoder_inputs_
   french_placeholder)
5.
6. decoder_lstm = LSTM(LSTM_NODES, return_sequences=True,
   return_state=True)
7. decoder_outputs, _, _ = decoder_lstm(decoder_inputs_x,
   initial_state=encoder_states)
8.
9. ###
10.
11. decoder_dense = Dense(num_words_output,
    activation='softmax')
12. decoder_outputs = decoder_dense(decoder_outputs)
```

The following script creates the complete training model for our seq2seq model.

Script 20:

```
1. model = Model([encoder_inputs_eng_placeholder,
2.   decoder_inputs_french_placeholder], decoder_outputs)
3. model.compile(
4.     optimizer='rmsprop',
5.     loss='categorical_crossentropy',
6.     metrics=['accuracy']
7. )
```

Execute the following script to display the training model.

Script 21:

```
1. from keras.utils import plot_model
2. plot_model(model, to_file='model_plot4a.png', show_
   shapes=True, show_layer_names=True)
```

Output:

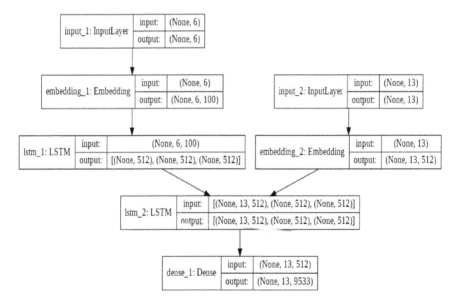

Finally, the following script trains the model.

Script 22:

```
1.  r = model.fit(
2.      [encoder_input_eng_sequences, decoder_input_french_
    sequences],
3.      decoder_one_hot_targets,
4.      batch_size=BATCH_SIZE,
5.      epochs=NUM_EPOCHS,
6.      validation_split=0.1,
7.  )
```

At the end of 20 epochs, an accuracy of around 79.67 is achieved.

Output:

```
Epoch 16/20
18000/18000 [==============================] - 23s 1ms/step
- loss: 0.4830 - accuracy: 0.9182 - val_loss: 1.4919 - val_
accuracy: 0.7976
Epoch 17/20
18000/18000 [==============================] - 23s 1ms/step
- loss: 0.4730 - accuracy: 0.9202 - val_loss: 1.5083 - val_
accuracy: 0.7962
Epoch 18/20
18000/18000 [==============================] - 23s 1ms/step
- loss: 0.4616 - accuracy: 0.9219 - val_loss: 1.5127 - val_
accuracy: 0.7963
Epoch 19/20
18000/18000 [==============================] - 22s 1ms/step
- loss: 0.4515 - accuracy: 0.9235 - val_loss: 1.5249 - val_
accuracy: 0.7963
Epoch 20/20
18000/18000 [==============================] - 23s 1ms/step
- loss: 0.4407 - accuracy: 0.9250 - val_loss: 1.5303 - val_
accuracy: 0.7967
```

11.2. Making Predictions Using Seq2Seq

You saw how to train a model in the previous section. In this section, you will see how to make predictions. The process of making predictions is elaborated by the following figure.

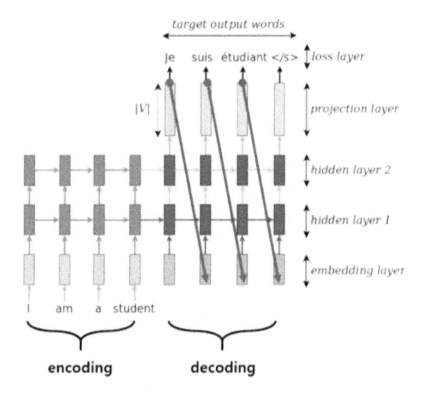

In the prediction phase, the input to the encoder is a complete sentence in its original language, just like the encoder. However, one of the inputs to the decoder is the hidden and cell states from the encoder. However, unlike the training phase, where the whole target sentence is fed as input simultaneously, during prediction at the first step, the word <sos> is fed as decoder input.

On the basis of the hidden and cell states and the first word <sos>, the decoder makes the prediction for the first translated word, which is "suis" in the above figure. At the second timestep, the input to the decoder is the hidden state and cell state from the first decoder timestep, and the output from the first decoder timestep, which is "Je." The process continues until the decoder predictions <eos>, which corresponds to the end of the sentence.

The following script implements the model for making predictions for translating text from English to French using the seq2seq model.

Script 23:

```
1. encoder_prediction_model = Model(encoder_inputs_eng_
   placeholder, encoder_states)
2.
3. decoder_state_input_h = Input(shape=(LSTM_NODES,))
4. decoder_state_input_c = Input(shape=(LSTM_NODES,))
5. decoder_states_inputs = [decoder_state_input_h, decoder_
   state_input_c]
6.
7.
8. decoder_inputs_single = Input(shape=(1,))
9. decoder_inputs_single_x = decoder_embedding(decoder_
   inputs_single)
10.
11.
12. decoder_outputs, h, c = decoder_lstm(decoder_inputs_
    single_x, initial_state=decoder_states_inputs)
13.
14.
15.
16. decoder_states = [h, c]
17. decoder_outputs = decoder_dense(decoder_outputs)
18.
19.
20. decoder_model = Model(
21.     [decoder_inputs_single] + decoder_states_inputs,
22.     [decoder_outputs] + decoder_states
23. )
```

The prediction model is plotted via the following script:

Script 24:

```
1. from keras.utils import plot_model
2. plot_model(model, to_file='model_plot4a.png', show_
   shapes=True, show_layer_names=True)
```

Output:

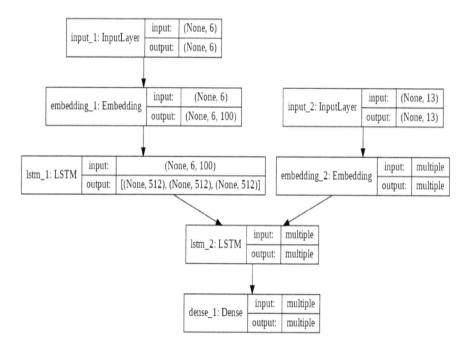

The prediction model makes the prediction in the form of integers, and you will need to convert the integers back to text. The following script creates an index to word dictionaries for both the input and output sentences.

Script 25:

```
idx2word_eng_input = {v:k for k, v in word2idx_eng_inputs.
items()}
idx2word_french_target = {v:k for k, v in word2idx_french_
outputs.items()}
```

In the following script, we create a "**perform_translation()**" method which accepts an input sequence of a sentence. The encoder encodes the input sequence and passes the hidden state and the cell state to the decoder. The first input to the decoder is the "sos" tag along with hidden and cell states from the encoder. A loop runs for maximum sentence length time.

During each iteration, a prediction is made. If the predicted word is "<eos>," the loop terminates. Else, using the predicted index, the actual word is found from the index to word dictionary, and the word is appended to the output sentence. The index and the hidden state and cell states of the decoder are updated, and the new values are used to make predictions using the decoder model again. The following script contains the code logic for the "**perform_translation()**" function.

Script 26:

```
1.  def perform_translation(input_seq):
2.      states_value = encoder_prediction_model.predict(input_
    seq)
3.      target_seq = np.zeros((1, 1))
4.      target_seq[0, 0] = word2idx_french_outputs['<sos>']
5.      eos = word2idx_french_outputs['<eos>']
6.      output_sentence = []
7.
8.      for _ in range(max_out_len):
9.          output_tokens, h, c = decoder_model.
    predict([target_seq] + states_value)
10.         idx = np.argmax(output_tokens[0, 0, :])
11.
12.         if eos == idx:
13.             break
14.
15.         word = ''
16.
17.         if idx > 0:
```

```
17.         if idx > 0:
18.             word = idx2word_french_target[idx]
19.             output_sentence.append(word)
20.
21.         target_seq[0, 0] = idx
22.         states_value = [h, c]
23.
24.     return ' '.join(output_sentence)
```

Now is the time to make predictions. The following script randomly chooses an input sentence from the list of input sentence sequences. The sentence sequence is passed to the "**perform_translation()**" method, which returns the translated sentence in French.

Script 27:

```
1. random_sentence_index = np.random.choice(len(input_
   english_sentences))
2. input_eng_seq = encoder_input_eng_sequences[random_
   sentence_index:random_sentence_index+1]
3. translation = perform_translation(input_eng_seq)
4. print('-')
5. print('Input Sentence:', input_english_sentences[random_
   sentence_index])
6. print('Translated Sentence:', translation)
```

The output shows that the sentence chosen randomly by our script is "You need sleep," which has been successfully translated into "vous avez besoin de sommeil" in French.

Output:

```
Input Sentence: You need sleep.
Translated Sentence: vous avez besoin de sommeil.
```

Further Readings – Seq2Seq Modeling

To study more about word seq2seq modeling, see these resources:

https://bit.ly/2Y8L9Zn
https://bit.ly/2ZkvmWI

Hands-on Time – Exercise

Now, it is your turn. Follow the instructions in **the exercises below** to check your understanding of seq2seq modeling with Keras. The answers to these questions are given at the end of the book.

Exercise 11.1

Question 1:

The process where ground truth value of the previous output is fed as input to the next timestep is called _____

    A. Truth Labelling

    B. Input Labelling

    C. Input Forcing

    D. Teacher Forcing

Question 2:

In seq2seq model, the input to the node in the decoder layer is _____

    A. Hidden state from the encoder

    B. Cell state from the encoder

    C. A "start of sentence" tag

    D. All of the above

Question 3:

To end predictions using decoder LSTM in seq2seq, what strategy is adopted?

    A. End sentence if maximum sentence length is achieved

    B. End sentence if "end of sentence" tag is predicted

    C. Both A and B

    D. None of the Above

Exercise 11.2

Using the spa.txt file from *data folder in the book resources*, create a seq2seq model for translating English sentences into Spanish.

12

State of the Art NLP with BERT Transformers

12.1. Introduction

Though word embeddings and recurrent neural networks such as LSTM have proven to be extremely efficient for various natural language processing tasks such as text classification, there are a few problems with LSTM and CNN based text classification systems.

With LSTM, data can only be read in a sequential manner in one direction. Though bidirectional LSTM solves this problem by reading data in both forward and backward directions, the text is still processed sequentially instead of being processed parallelly. This is where transformer models come into play. Transformer models process the whole text document in parallel, relying on attention mechanism.

In the attention mechanism, instead of processing text sequentially, the text is processed in parallel, which allows the attention systems to assign weightage to important parts of the text in a parallel manner.

Several transformer models have been developed until now. However, in this chapter, you will be studying BERT, which stands for (Bidirectional Encoder Representations from Transformers) developed by Google.

12.2. Why Use BERT?

A question that should come to your mind is, why should we use BERT over traditional word embeddings and LSTM based neural networks?

The answer to this question is that BERT models are able to generate word representations that capture local context. For instance, with word embeddings, the representation of the word "apple" will be the same even if we talk about "apple I phone" or apple as a fruit. With BERT, a different word representation will be generated. In addition, BERT models divide words into stems and leaf segments. For instance, the word "Judgmental" is treated as two separate tokens "Judgement" and "al," which makes word representation more flexible.

12.3. BERT Text Classification Steps

Normally, the BERT model is used for generating text representations, which you can then use with LSTM or CNN networks to build text classification or any other type of model. However, BERT also contains Sequence Classification models, which can be used to classify text.

The steps involved in text classification using BERT sequence models are as follows:

1. In the first step, you have to generate BERT tokens. To do so, you can use the BERT Tokenizer.

2. The second step is to convert data into the format that can be used by a BERT model and perform word embeddings using BERT.

3. Create a sequence classification model for BERT.

4. Train the sequence classification model.

5. Evaluate the model on the test set.

12.4. BERT Tokenization and Embeddings

In this section, you will see how to perform tokenization using BERT tokenizer. BERT model expects data in a 3-dimensional format containing the input ids, the attention masks, and the token type ids. You will see these properties in detail later in this section.

You will be using the transformers library from Hugging Face. The transformers library can be installed via the following script.

```
! pip install transformers
```

Next, to tokenize the texts, we need to import the BertTokenizer class from the transformers module, as shown below:

Script 1:

```
from transformers import BertTokenizer
```

The fast way is to load pretrained word embeddings for tokenizers. The following script creates a BERT tokenizer object with pretrained embeddings. Next, we define a sample sentence and set the maximum sentence length to 25.

Script 2:

```
1. bert_tokenizer = BertTokenizer.from_pretrained('bert-base-
   uncased', do_lower_case=True)
2. max_sent_length = 25
3. sample_sent = 'Hello, are you judgemental. No I am
   incremental.'
```

To tokenize a sentence, you can use the `tokenize()` method of the BERT tokenizer, as shown below. Also, with BERT, each sentence should be prefixed with a "[CLS]" tag and ended with a "[SEP]" tag as shown below:

Script 3:

```
1. sample_sent_plus_special_tokens = '[CLS]' + sample_sent +
   '[SEP]'
2. tokenized_sent = bert_tokenizer.tokenize(sample_sent_plus_
   special_tokens)
3. print('tokenized_sent', tokenized_sent)
```

The following output shows a tokenized sentence.

Output:

```
tokenized_sent ['[CLS]', 'hello', ',', 'are', 'you',
'judgement', '##al', '.', 'no', 'i', 'am', 'inc', '##rem',
'##ental', '.', '[SEP]']
```

Next, you need to convert the text tokens into the integer format. To do so, you can use the `convert_tokens_to_ids()` method of the BERT tokenizer, as shown below:

Script 4:

```
1. input_ids = bert_tokenizer.convert_tokens_to_
   ids(tokenized_sent)
2. print(input_ids)
```

The ids for the words in the sample input sentence are as follows.

Output:

```
[101, 7592, 1010, 2024, 2017, 16646, 2389, 1012, 2053, 1045,
2572, 4297, 28578, 21050, 1012, 102]
```

We need to apply padding to the input sentences so that all the sentences have the same length. The following script calculates the pad length for the sample sentence. Since the maximum sentence length is set to 25 and the input sentence contains 16 tokens, the pad length will be 9, as shown below:

Script 5:

```
1.  pad_length = max_sent_length - len(input_ids)
2.  print(pad_length)
```

Output:

```
9
```

The following script adds 9 0s at the end of the input ids token ids.

Script 6:

```
1.  input_ids = input_ids + ([0] * pad_length)
2.  print(input_ids))
```

Output:

```
[101, 7592, 1010, 2024, 2017, 16646, 2389, 1012, 2053, 1045,
2572, 4297, 28578, 21050, 1012, 102, 0, 0, 0, 0, 0, 0, 0, 0, 0]
```

Attention masks are a list of 0s and 1s where a 1 is added to the positions that contained original objects, while 0 is added to the padding indexes.

Script 7:

```
1.  att_mask = [1] * len(input_ids)
2.  att_mask = att_mask+ ([0] * pad_length)
3.  print(att_mask)
```

Output:

```
[1, 1, 1, 1, 1, 1, 1, 1, 1, 1, 1, 1, 1, 1, 1, 1, 1, 1, 1, 1,
1, 1, 1, 1, 1, 0, 0, 0, 0, 0, 0, 0, 0, 0]
```

Token type ids are used to separate input sentence from an output sentence in case there are two sentences in the input. Zeros are added for the index of the first sentence, while a 1 is added for the indexes of the other sentence. Since we have only a single sentence, we will only create a list of all Os for token type ids.

Script 8:

```
token_type_ids = [0] * max_sent_length
```

Finally, to create a complete input for BERT models, a dictionary of token ids, token type ids, and attention mask is created, as shown below.

Script 9:

```
1. input_for_bert = {
2.     "token_ids": input_ids,
3.     "token_type_ids": token_type_ids,
4.     "attention_mask": att_mask
5. }
6. print(input_for_bert)
```

Output:

```
{'token_ids': [101, 7592, 1010, 2024, 2017, 16646, 2389, 1012,
2053, 1045, 2572, 4297, 28578, 21050, 1012, 102, 0, 0, 0, 0,
0, 0, 0, 0, 0], 'token_type_ids': [0, 0, 0, 0, 0, 0, 0, 0, 0,
0, 0, 0, 0, 0, 0, 0, 0, 0, 0, 0, 0, 0, 0, 0, 0], 'attention_
mask': [1, 1, 1, 1, 1, 1, 1, 1, 1, 1, 1, 1, 1, 1, 1, 1, 1, 1,
1, 1, 1, 1, 1, 1, 1, 0, 0, 0, 0, 0, 0, 0, 0, 0]}
```

Instead of creating input data in a correct format manually, you can simply use the encode_plus function of the BertTokenizer object as shown below:

Script 10:

```
1.  input_for_bert= bert_tokenizer.encode_plus(
2.                      sample_sent,
3.                      add_special_tokens = True,
4.                      max_length = max_sent_length,
5.                      pad_to_max_length = True,
6.                      return_attention_mask = True,
7.              )
8.  print('encoded', input_for_bert)
```

The following output is similar to what we achieved when we prepared BERT input data manually.

Output:

```
Truncation was not explicitly activated but `max_length` is
provided a specific value, please use `truncation=True` to
explicitly truncate examples to max length. Defaulting to
'longest_first' truncation strategy. If you encode pairs of
sequences (GLUE-style) with the tokenizer you can select this
strategy more precisely by providing a specific strategy to
`truncation`.
encoded {'input_ids': [101, 7592, 1010, 2024, 2017, 16646,
2389, 1012, 2053, 1045, 2572, 4297, 28578, 21050, 1012, 102,
0, 0, 0, 0, 0, 0, 0, 0, 0], 'token_type_ids': [0, 0, 0, 0, 0,
0, 0, 0, 0, 0, 0, 0, 0, 0, 0, 0, 0, 0, 0, 0, 0, 0, 0, 0, 0],
'attention_mask': [1, 1, 1, 1, 1, 1, 1, 1, 1, 1, 1, 1, 1, 1,
1, 1, 0, 0, 0, 0, 0, 0, 0, 0, 0]}
```

12.5. Text Classification with BERT

In the previous chapters, you saw how machine learning and simple LSTM can be used for text classification. In this section, we will be using BERT to perform the classification of IDMB movie reviews into positive or negative reviews.

The following script imports the required module and makes sure that Google Colab's GPU is being used. Remember, BERT transformers take a lot of time to train. So, always try to execute them on GPU or even TPUs.

Script 11:

```
1.  import numpy as np
2.
3.  import tensorflow as tf
4.  import tensorflow_hub as hub
5.  import tensorflow_datasets as tfds
6.
7.  import matplotlib.pyplot as plt
8.
9.  print("Version: ", tf.__version__)
10. print("Eager mode: ", tf.executing_eagerly())
11. print("Hub version: ", hub.__version__)
12. print("GPU is", "available" if tf.test.is_gpu_available()
    else "NOT AVAILABLE")
```

The following script imports the Google Drive that contains our data.

Script 12:

```
1.  from google.colab import drive
2.  drive.mount('/gdrive')
```

Similarly, the following script imports the IDMB dataset and displays its header.

Script 13:

```
1.  import pandas as pd
2.  import numpy as np
3.  import re
4.  import nltk
5.  from nltk.corpus import stopwords
6.
7.  imdb_data= pd.read_csv("/gdrive/My Drive/datasets/IMDB
    Dataset.csv")
8.
9.  imdb_data.head()
```

Output:

	review	sentiment
0	One of the other reviewers has mentioned that ...	positive
1	A wonderful little production. The...	positive
2	I thought this was a wonderful way to spend ti...	positive
3	Basically there's a family where a little boy ...	negative
4	Petter Mattei's "Love in the Time of Money" is...	positive

We need to clean the text reviews as it contains HTML tags and special characters. The following method defines the clean_text() method, which cleans the text reviews.

Script 14:

```
1.  def clean_text(doc):
2.
3.      document = remove_tags(doc)
4.
5.      document = re.sub('[^a-zA-Z]', ' ', document)
6.
7.      document = re.sub(r"\s+[a-zA-Z]\s+", ' ', document)
8.
9.      document = re.sub(r'\s+', ' ', document)
```

```
10.
11.      return document
12.
13. TAG_RE = re.compile(r'<[^>]+>')
14.
15. def remove_tags(document):
16.      return TAG_RE.sub('', document)
```

The following script cleans text reviews and replaces positive and negative sentiment in the sentiment column by 1 and 0, respectively.

Script 15:

```
1.  imdb_data["review"] = imdb_data["review"].apply(clean_
    text)
2.  imdb_data['sentiment'] = imdb_data['sentiment'].
    map({'positive': 1,'negative': 0})
3.  imdb_data.head()
```

Here is how the dataset looks after data cleaning and converting sentiment values to 1s and 0s.

Output:

	review	sentiment
0	One of the other reviewers has mentioned that ...	1
1	A wonderful little production The filming tech...	1
2	I thought this was wonderful way to spend time...	1
3	Basically there a family where little boy Jake...	0
4	Petter Mattei Love in the Time of Money is vis...	1

Let's now install the **transformers** library from Hugging Face.

Script 16:

```
! pip install transformers
```

Import TFBertForSequenceClassification and BertToknizer classes from the transformers library using the following script.

Script 17:

```
1. from sklearn import preprocessing
2. from sklearn.model_selection import train_test_split
3.
4.
5. from transformers import (TFBertForSequenceClassification,
6.                           BertTokenizer)
7.
8. from tqdm import tqdm
```

The following script divides the data into the training set and test set.

Script 18:

```
1. X = imdb_data['review'].values
2. y = imdb_data['sentiment'].values
3.
4. X_train, X_test, y_train, y_test = train_test_split(X, y,
   test_size=0.2, random_state=42)
5.
6. print("Shape of training data: {0}, \nShape of test data:
   {1}".format(X_train.shape, X_test.shape))
```

Output:

```
1. Shape of training data: (40000,),
2. Shape of test data: (10000,)
```

The above output shows that 40,000 reviews will be used for training, while 10,000 reviews will be used to test the classification model.

Let's create an object of the BertTokenizer class.

Script 19:

```
bert_tokenizer = BertTokenizer.from_pretrained("bert-base-
cased")
```

As explained in the Tokenization section, the input to a BERT model is 3-dimensional and consists of input ids, token type ids, and the attention masks. The following defines text_to_bert_input() method, which accepts plain text and returns a list of input ids, token type ids, and attention masks. The max_length is 128, which means that only the first 128 words of each review will be used for classification.

Script 20:

```
1.  pad_token=0
2.  pad_token_segment_id=0
3.  max_length= 128
4.
5.  def text_to_bert_input(reviews):
6.      input_ids,attention_masks,token_type_ids=[],[],[]
7.
8.      for review in tqdm(reviews,position=0, leave=True):
9.          bert_inputs = bert_tokenizer.encode_plus(review,add_
        special_tokens=True, max_length=max_length, truncation =
        True)
10.
11.         input, token_type = bert_inputs["input_ids"], bert_
        inputs["token_type_ids"]
12.         mask = [1] * len(input)
13.
14.         padding_length = max_length - len(input)
15.
16.         input = input + ([pad_token] * padding_length)
17.         mask = mask + ([0] * padding_length)
18.         token_type  = token_type  + ([pad_token_segment_id] *
        padding_length)
19.
20.         input_ids.append(input)
```

```
21.      attention_masks.append(mask)
22.      token_type_ids.append(token_type)
23.
24.   return [np.asarray(input_ids),
25.             np.asarray(attention_masks),
26.             np.asarray(token_type_ids)]
```

The following script calls the text_to_bert_input() method and converts the training set and test set into a format that can be used as inputs to the BERT models.

Script 21:

```
1.  X_test_input=text_to_bert_input(X_test)
2.  X_train_input=text_to_bert_input(X_train)
```

Since we are using the TensorFlow backend to train BERT models, we need to convert the input data into tensors. The following script does that for both the training and test sets.

Script 22:

```
1.  def convert_to_tensors(input_ids,attention_masks,token_
    type_ids,y):
2.    return {"input_ids": input_ids,
3.             "attention_mask": attention_masks,
4.             "token_type_ids": token_type_ids},y
5.
6.
7.  train_dataset = tf.data.Dataset.from_tensor_slices((X_
    train_input[0],X_train_input[1],X_train_input[2],y_
    train)).map(convert_to_tensors).shuffle(100).batch(32)
8.
9.  test_dataset = tf.data.Dataset.from_tensor_slices((X_
    test_input[0],X_test_input[1],X_test_input[2],y_test)).
    map(convert_to_tensors).batch(64)
```

Next, you need to define the classification model. With Hugging Face's transformers library, you can use the TFBertForSequenceClassificaion class to create a text classification model. The process of defining loss, optimizer, and evaluation metrics is similar to any other TensorFlow model. The following script creates a BERT text classification model and displays the model summary in the output.

Script 23:

```
1. model = TFBertForSequenceClassification.from_
   pretrained("bert-base-cased")
2.
3. optimizer = tf.keras.optimizers.Adam(learning_rate=3e-5,
   epsilon=1e-08)
4. loss = tf.keras.losses.SparseCategoricalCrossentropy(from_
   logits=True)
5. metric = tf.keras.metrics.
   SparseCategoricalAccuracy('accuracy')
6.
7. model.compile(optimizer=optimizer, loss=loss,
   metrics=[metric])
8.
9. model.summary()
```

Output:

Layer (type)	Output Shape	Param #
bert (TFBertMainLayer) 108310272	multiple	
dropout_37 (Dropout)	multiple	0
classifier (Dense)	multiple	1538

```
Total params: 108,311,810
Trainable params: 108,311,810
Non-trainable params: 0
```

Finally, you can call fit on the model object to train the BERT sequence classification model.

Script 24:

```
history = model.fit(train_dataset, epochs=1, validation_
data=test_dataset)
```

Output:

```
1250/1250 [==============================] - 1358s 1s/step
- loss: 0.3178 - accuracy: 0.8621 - val_loss: 0.2466 - val_
accuracy: 0.8969
```

The output shows that a maximum accuracy of 89.69 is achieved using the BERT classifier after only one epoch. In chapter 8, section 1, the random forest algorithm was used to predict the movie sentiment of the IMDB dataset, which achieved a test accuracy of 83.5. In chapter 10, section 2, a convolutional neural network was used for the classification of IMBD reviews, which returned an accuracy of 80.78 percent. The accuracy achieved via BERT is greater than both the baselines and that too, using only the first 128 words of the sequence.

Further Readings – BERT

To study more about word BERT for text classification, take a look at these links:

https://bit.ly/3imHI9w
https://bit.ly/2BrBPYg
https://bit.ly/31Jsg1d

Hands-on Time – Exercise

Now, it is your turn. Follow the instructions in **the exercises below** to check your understanding of BERT. The answers to these questions are given at the end of the book.

Exercise 12.1

Question 1:

To convert data into the BERT input format, which function can be used from the BertTokenizer class?

    A. encode

    B. encode_plus

    C. encode_bert

    D. A and B

Question 2:

BERT models are capable of capturing:

    A. Text Similarity

    B. Global Context Information

    C. Local Context Information

    D. All of the above

Question 3:

The transformers library from Hugging Face contains BERT models that cannot be used for:

    A. Image Classification

    B. Text Classification

    C. Both A and B

    D. None of the Above

Exercise 12.2

Using the "ham_spam.csv" file from Resources/Data, develop a BERT-based sequence classifier.

Hands-on NLP Projects/ Articles for Practice

This section contains some of the most interesting NLP-based projects and competitions that you can try on your own.

1. **Text Classification**

    1.1. Toxic Comment Classification Challenge (https://bit.ly/38tRjGV)

    1.2. TensorFlow Hub for Text Classification (https://bit.ly/2VG8GPR)

    1.3. Medical Symptoms Text & Audio Classification (https://bit.ly/3gszpY8)

2. **Topic Modeling**

    2.1. Topic Modeling: Finding Related Articles (https://bit.ly/2NXgUi5)

    2.2. Topic Modeling on Quora Insincere Questions (https://bit.ly/31IPh4t)

    2.3. TED Talks topic models (https://bit.ly/2ZzpvwU)

3. Seq2Seq Modeling

3.1. Text Summarization with Seq2Seq Model
(https://bit.ly/3isq8AZ)

3.2. Signal prediction with a seq2seq RNN
(https://bit.ly/38zmaCg)

3.3. Seq2seq chatbot keras with attention
(https://bit.ly/2C1FfRg)

4. BERT and its Applications

4.1. Topic Modeling BERT+LDA
(https://bit.ly/38oRqUq)

4.2. TensorFlow 2.0 - Bert YES/NO Answers
(https://bit.ly/2VK6QgX)

4.3. BERT for Humans: Tutorial+Baseline
(https://bit.ly/3fbljtG)

From the Same Publisher

Python Machine Learning
https://bit.ly/3gcb2iG

Python Deep Learning
https://bit.ly/3gci9Ys

Python Data Visualization
https://bit.ly/3wXqDJI

Python for Data Analysis
https://bit.ly/3wPYEM2

Python Data Preprocessing

https://bit.ly/3fLV3ci

Python for NLP

https://bit.ly/3chlTqm

10 ML Projects Explained from Scratch

https://bit.ly/34KFsDk

Python Scikit-Learn for Beginners

https://bit.ly/3fPbtRf

Data Science
with Python
https://bit.ly/3wVQ5iN

Statistics
with Python
https://bit.ly/3z27KHt

Exercise Solutions

Exercise 1

Question 1:

Which of the following is not an application of NLP?

    A. Image Labeling

    B. Poetry Generation

    C. Sentimental Analysis

    D. Email Classification

Answer: A

Question 2:

Which of the following is not an NLP task?

    A. Tokenization

    B. Stop Word Removal

    C. Parts of Speech Tagging

    D. Image Segmentation

Answer: D

Question 3:

Which of the following is not a disadvantage of rule-based approaches for NLP?

A. Not Flexible

B. Not Scalable

C. Require Huge Dataset

D. None of the Above

Answer: C

Exercise 2.1

Question 1

Which iteration should be used when you want to repeatedly execute a code specific number of times?

A. For Loop

B. While Loop

C. Both A and B

D. None of the above

Answer: A

Question 2

What is the maximum number of values that a function can return in Python?

A. Single Value

B. Double Value

C. More than two values

D. None

Answer: C

Question 3

Which of the following membership operators are supported by Python?

    A. In

    B. Out

    C. Not In

    D. Both A and C

Answer: D

Exercise 2.2

Print the table of integer 9 using a while loop:

```
1.  j=1
2.  while j< 11:
3.      print("9 x "+str(j)+ " = "+ str(9*j))
4.      j=j+1
```

Exercise 3.1

Question 1:

In a neural network with three input features, one hidden layer of five nodes, and an output layer of three possible values, what will be the dimensions of weights that connect the input to the hidden layer? Remember, the dimensions of the input data are (m,3), where m is the number of records.

    A. [5,3]

    B. [3,5]

    C. [4,5]

    D. [5,4]

Answer B:

Question 2:

The pooling layer is used to pick correct features even if:

    A. Image is inverted

    B. Image is distorted

    C. Image is compressed

    D. All of the above

Answer: D

Question 3:

The shape of the feature set passed to the LSTM's input layer should be:

    A. Number of Records, Features, Timesteps

    B. Timesteps, Features, Number of Records

    C. Features, Timesteps, Number of Records

    D. Number of Records, Timesteps, Features

Answer: D

Exercise 3.2

Using the CFAR 10 image dataset, perform image classification to recognize. Here is the dataset:

```
cifar_dataset = tf.keras.datasets.cifar10
```

Solution:

```
(training_images, training_labels), (test_images, test_labels)
= cifar_dataset.load_data()

training_images, test_images = training_images/255.0,
test_images/255.0
```

```
training_labels, test_labels = training_labels.flatten(),
test_labels.flatten()
print(training_labels.shape)
print(training_images.shape)

output_classes = len(set(training_labels))
print("Number of output classes is: ", output_classes)

input_layer = Input(shape = training_images[0].shape)
conv1 = Conv2D(32, (3,3), strides = 2, activation= 'relu')
(input_layer)

maxpool1 = MaxPool2D(2, 2)(conv1)

conv2 = Conv2D(64, (3,3), strides = 2, activation= 'relu')
(maxpool1)

#conv3 = Conv2D(128, (3,3), strides = 2, activation= 'relu')
(conv2)

flat1 = Flatten()(conv2)

drop1 = Dropout(0.2)(flat1)

dense1 = Dense(512, activation = 'relu')(drop1)
drop2  = Dropout(0.2)(dense1)

output_layer = Dense(output_classes, activation= 'softmax')
(drop2)

model = Model(input_layer, output_layer)

model.compile(optimizer = 'adam', loss= 'sparse_categorical_
crossentropy', metrics =['accuracy'])
model_history = model.fit(training_images, training_labels,
epochs=20, validation_data=(test_images, test_labels),
verbose=1)
```

Exercise 4.1

Consider the following sentence:

```
sentence = "Nick's car was sold for $ 1500".
```

Perform the following tasks on the above sentence:

1. Replace special characters with empty spaces
2. Remove multiple empty spaces and replace them by a single space
3. Remove any single character
4. Convert the text to all lower case
5. Split the text to individual words

Solution:

```
sentence = "Nick's car was sold for $ 1500."

sentence = re.sub(r"[^\w ]", " ", sentence, flags =re.I)
print(sentence)

sentence = re.sub(r"\s+", " ", sentence, flags =re.I)
print(sentence)

sentence  = re.sub(r"\s+[a-zA-Z]\s+", " ", sentence)
print(sentence)

sentence = sentence.lower()
print(sentence)

sentence = sentence.split(" ")
print(sentence)
```

Exercise 4.2

Question 1:

To remove special characters from a string, which regular expression can be used?

    A. re.sub(r"[^\w]", "", sentence, flags =re.I)

    B. re.sub(r"[^a-zA-z0-9]", "", sentence, flags =re.I)

    C. Both A and B

    D. None of the Above

Answer: C

Question 2:

To find if a string exists in another substring, we can use:

    A. contains operator

    B. exist operator

    C. in operator

    D. substring operator

Answer: C

Question 3:

Which regular expression is used to match any string with at least one character?

    A. re.match(r".*", sentence)

    B. re.match(r".+", sentence)

    C. re.match(r".-", sentence)

    D. re.match(r"./", sentence)

Answer: B

Exercise 5.1

Remove special characters and digits from the following text and then perform stop word removal and tokenize. Finally, print the output. You can take help from chapter 4 to remove special characters and digits.

Note: The following text is obtained from the first two paragraphs of the Wikipedia's article on Machine Learning:

```
text = """"Machine learning (ML) is the study of computer
algorithms that improve automatically through experience.[1]
It is seen as a subset of artificial intelligence. Machine
learning algorithms build a mathematical model based on sample
data,
known as "training data",
in order to make predictions or decisions without being
explicitly programmed to do so.[2][3]:2 Machine learning
algorithms are
used in a wide variety of applications, such as email filtering
and computer vision, where it is difficult or infeasible to
develop conventional algorithms to perform the needed tasks.

Machine learning is closely related to computational
statistics, which focuses on making predictions using
computers.
The study of mathematical optimization delivers methods,
theory and application domains to the field of machine
learning.
Data mining is a related field of study, focusing on
exploratory data analysis through unsupervised learning.[4][5]
In its application across business problems, machine learning
is also referred to as predictive analytics."""
```

Solution:

```
import re
from nltk.corpus import stopwords
nltk.download('stopwords')
from nltk.tokenize import word_tokenize

text = re.sub(r"[^a-z ]", "", text, flags =re.I)

word_tokens = word_tokenize(text)

text_without_stopwords = [word for word in word_tokens if not
word in stopwords.words()]

print(text_without_stopwords)
```

Exercise 5.2

Question 1:

Which NLTK function is used to divide a sentence into individual words?

   A. text_tokenize()

   B. word_tokenize()

   C. tokenize()

   D. None of the Above

Answer: B

Question 2:

Which POS tag represents named entities?

   A. NNP

   B. NP

   C. PP

   D. NE

Answer: A

Question 3:

Word sense disambiguation is used when:

   A. A word has the same meaning in multiple sentences

   B. A word has different meanings in multiple sentences

   C. A word is the opposite of another word

   D. None of the above

Answer: B

Exercise 6.1

Question 1:

Which delimiter is used to read the TSV file with the Pandas read_csv method?

   A. sep ='tab'

   B. sep = ' '

   C. sep ='\t'

   D. None of the Above

Answer: C

Question 2:

Which Python module is used to import data from SQL Server?

A. SqlAlchemy

B. pyodbc

C. sqlite3

D. None of the Above

Answer: B

Question 3:

Which function is used to convert a database table to a Pandas dataframe?

A. pd.read_sql_query

B. pd.read_sql

C. pd.read_csv

D. pd.read_tsv

Answer: A

Exercise 6.2

In the *data folder of the book resources*, you will find a file CSV *airline_review*. Read the CSV file, and print the first five reviews. You can use the head method of the Pandas dataframe for that purpose.

Solution:

```
1.  import pandas as pd
2.  airline_csv = pd.read_csv(r"E:\Datasets\airline_review.
    csv", encoding = "utf-8")
3.  for i in range(5):
4.      print(airline_csv["text"][i])
```

Exercise 7.1

Question 1:

Which of the following is not a disadvantage of the Bag of Words and NGrams approaches?

    A. Results in a huge sparse matrix

    B. Context information is not retained

    C. Requires a huge amount of data to train

    D. None of the above

Answer: C

Question 2:

Which attribute is used to specify the range of N-Grams via Sklearn's CountVectorizer?

    A. ngrams

    B. ng_rage

    C. ngrams_range

    D. ngram_range

Answer: D

Question 3:

Suppose you develop a custom word2vec model "GensimModel" with Gensim. How will you display words similar to "Machine"?

    A. GensimModel.wv.most_similar("Machine")

    B. GensimModel.most_similar("Machine")

    C. GensimModel.wv.similar("Machine")

    D. GensimModel.similar("Machine")

Answer: A

Exercise 7.2

Using the following corpus, create bag of words and TF-IDF models without stop words. Display the original words and the bag of words and TF-IDF vectors:

```
12. dataset = [
13.
14.     'This movie is excellent',
15.     'I loved the movie, it was fantastic',
16.     'The film is brilliant, you should watch',
17.     'Wonderful movie',
18.     'one of the best films ever',
19.     'fantastic film to watch',
20.     'great movie',
21.     'Acting and direction is brilliant'
22. ]
```

Solution:

```
1.  ## Bag of Words Approach
2.
3.  from sklearn.feature_extraction.text import
    CountVectorizer
4.  bog_vectorizer = CountVectorizer(stop_words='english')
5.
6.  bog_vectorizer.fit(dataset)
7.
8.  bog_vectors =  bog_vectorizer.transform(dataset)
9.  for i in range(len(dataset)):
10.     print(dataset[i],"-->",bog_vectors[i].toarray())
11.
12.
13. ## TFIDF Approach
14.
15. from sklearn.feature_extraction.text import TfidfVectorizer
16. tfidf_vectorizer = TfidfVectorizer(stop_words='english')
17.
18. tfidf_vectorizer.fit(dataset)
19.
```

```
20. tfidf_vectors =   tfidf_vectorizer.transform(dataset)
21. for i in range(len(dataset)):
22.     print(dataset[i],"-->",tfidf_vectors[i].toarray())
```

Exercise 8.1

Question 1:

Which attribute of the TfidfVectorizer vectorizer is used to define the minimum word count?

    A. min_word

    B. min_count

    C. min_df

    D. None of the Above

Answer: C

Question 2:

Which method of the RandomForestClassifier object is used to train the algorithm on the input data?

    A. train()

    B. fit()

    C. predict()

    D. train_data()

Answer: B

Question 3:

Sentimental analysis with RandomForestClassifier is a type of
___ learning problem.

    A. Supervised

    B. Unsupervised

    C. Reinforcement

    D. Lazy

Answer: A

Exercise 8.2

Use CountVectorizer to perform sentimental analysis of
the "imdb_reviews.csv" dataset available in the *Resources/
Datasets* folder of this book. See if you can get better
performance with CountVectorizer compared to the
TfidfVectorizer.

Solution:

```
1.  import numpy as np
2.  import pandas as pd
3.  import re
4.  import nltk
5.  import matplotlib.pyplot as plt
6.  import seaborn as sns
7.  %matplotlib inline
8.
9.  data_path = "E:/Datasets/imdb_reviews.csv"
10. movie_dataset = pd.read_csv(data_path, engine='python')
11.
12. X = movie_dataset["SentimentText"]
13.
14. y = movie_dataset["Sentiment"]
15.
16. def clean_text(doc):
```

```
17.
18.
19.     document = re.sub('[^a-zA-Z]', ' ', doc)
20.
21.     document = re.sub(r"\s+[a-zA-Z]\s+", ' ', document)
22.
23.     document = re.sub(r'\s+', ' ', document)
24.
25.     return document
26.
27. X_sentences = []
28. reviews = list(X)
29. for rev in reviews:
30.     X_sentences.append(clean_text(rev))
31.
32.
33. from nltk.corpus import stopwords
34. from sklearn.feature_extraction.text import
    CountVectorizer
35.
36. vectorizer = CountVectorizer (max_features=2000, min_df=5,
    max_df=0.7, stop_words=stopwords.words('english'))
37. X= vectorizer.fit_transform(X_sentences).toarray()
38.
39. from sklearn.model_selection import train_test_split
40. X_train, X_test, y_train, y_test = train_test_split(X, y,
    test_size=0.20, random_state=42)
41.
42.
43. from sklearn.ensemble import RandomForestClassifier
44.
45. clf = RandomForestClassifier(n_estimators=250, random_
    state=0)
46. clf.fit(X_train, y_train)
47.
48. y_pred = clf.predict(X_test)
49.
50. from sklearn.metrics import classification_report,
    confusion_matrix, accuracy_score
```

```
51.
52. print(confusion_matrix(y_test,y_pred))
53. print(classification_report(y_test,y_pred))
54. print(accuracy_score(y_test,y_pred))
```

Exercise 9.1

Question 1:

The type of text summary that includes contents from the original text is called:

    A. Abstractive Summary

    B. Extractive Summary

    C. Derived Summary

    D. None of the Above

Answer: B

Question 2:

To parse a Wikipedia page, which of the following attribute of the `page` object is used?

    A. text

    B. data

    C. content

    D. raw_data

Answer: C

Question 3:

To create Gensim corpora, you need to pass a collection of tokens to which object:

    A. gensim.Corpora()

    B. gensim.Corpus()

    C. gensim.Collection()

    D. gensim.Dictionary()

Answer: D

Exercise 9.2

Using Wikipedia Library for Python, perform text summarization of the Wikipedia article on Coronavirus. Add only sentences that contain less than 40 words. Display the first 10 sentences from the summary.

Solution:

```
1.  import wikipedia
2.  import nltk
3.  import re
4.  from nltk.stem import WordNetLemmatizer
5.
6.  stemmer = WordNetLemmatizer()
7.
8.  nltk.download('stopwords')
9.  en_stop = set(nltk.corpus.stopwords.words('english'))
10.
11. covid = wikipedia.page("Corona Virus")
12.
13. scrapped_data = covid.content
14.
15. scrapped_data = re.sub(r'\[[0-9]*\]', ' ',  scrapped_data)
16. scrapped_data = re.sub(r'\s+', ' ',  scrapped_data)
17.
```

```
18. formatted_text = re.sub('[^a-zA-Z]', ' ', scrapped_data)
19. formatted_text = re.sub(r'\s+', ' ', formatted_text)
20.
21. import nltk
22. all_sentences = nltk.sent_tokenize(scrapped_data)
23.
24. stopwords = nltk.corpus.stopwords.words('english')
25.
26. word_freq = {}
27. for word in nltk.word_tokenize(formatted_text):
28.     if word not in stopwords:
29.         if word not in word_freq.keys():
30.             word_freq[word] = 1
31.         else:
32.             word_freq[word] += 1
33.
34. max_freq = max(word_freq.values())
35.
36. for word in word_freq.keys():
37.     word_freq[word] = (word_freq[word]/max_freq)
38.
39. sentence_scores = {}
40. for sentence in all_sentences:
41.     for token in nltk.word_tokenize(sentence.lower()):
42.         if token in word_freq.keys():
43.             if len(sentence.split(' ')) < 40:
44.                 if sentence not in sentence_scores.keys():
45.                     sentence_scores[sentence] = word_
    freq[token]
46.                 else:
47.                     sentence_scores[sentence] += word_
    freq[token]
48.
49. import heapq
50. selected_sentences= heapq.nlargest(10, sentence_scores,
    key=sentence_scores.get)
51.
52. text_summary = ' '.join(selected_sentences)
53. print(text_summary)
```

Exercise 10.1

Question 1

Which of the following is not a pretrained word embedding?

    A. Glove

    B. Stanford

    C. Peeking

    D. All of the above

Answer: C

Question 2

What should be the first argument to the Keras Embedding Layer?

    A. The input vector dimensions

    B. The output vector dimensions

    C. The word embedding size

    D. The vocabulary size

Answer: D

Question 3

Which layer will you need to use if you want to directly connect the Embedding Layer with a Dense Layer?

    A. LSTM layer with return_sequence set to False

    B. CNN layer with max pooling

    C. Flatten layer

    D. None of the Above

Answer: C

Exercise 10.2

Using the ***airline_review.csv*** dataset that we used for sentiment classification in section 10.1, perform classification using a DNN (Densely Connected Neural Network).

See if you can get better results with DNN as compared to the results in section 10.1.

Solution:

```
1.  import pandas as pd
2.  import numpy as np
3.  import re
4.  import nltk
5.  from nltk.corpus import stopwords
6.
7.  from numpy import array
8.  from tensorflow.keras.preprocessing.text import one_hot
9.  from tensorflow.keras.preprocessing.sequence import pad_
    sequences
10. from tensorflow.keras.models import Sequential
11. from tensorflow.keras.layers import Activation, LSTM,
    Dropout, Dense, Flatten, Input,  Embedding, Conv1D, Input
12. from tensorflow.keras.models import Model
13. from sklearn.model_selection import train_test_split
14. from tensorflow.keras.preprocessing.text import Tokenizer
15. from google.colab import drive
16. drive.mount('/gdrive')
17.
18. airline_data = pd.read_csv("/gdrive/My Drive/datasets/
    airline_review.csv")
19. airline_data.head()
20.
21.
22. X = airline_data["text"]
23.
24. y = pd.get_dummies(airline_data.airline_sentiment,
    prefix='sent').values
```

```
25.
26. def clean_text(doc):
27.
28.     document = remove_tags(doc)
29.
30.     document = re.sub('[^a-zA-Z]', ' ', document)
31.
32.     document = re.sub(r"\s+[a-zA-Z]\s+", ' ', document)
33.
34.     document = re.sub(r'\s+', ' ', document)
35.
36.     return document
37. TAG_RE = re.compile(r'<[^>]+>')
38.
39. def remove_tags(document):
40.     return TAG_RE.sub('', document)
41. X_sentences = []
42. reviews = list(X)
43. for rev in reviews:
44.     X_sentences.append(clean_text(rev))
45. X_train, X_test, y_train, y_test = train_test_split(X_
    sentences, y, test_size=0.20, random_state=42)
46. tokenizer = Tokenizer(num_words=5000)
47. tokenizer.fit_on_texts(X_train)
48.
49. X_train = tokenizer.texts_to_sequences(X_train)
50. X_test = tokenizer.texts_to_sequences(X_test)
51. vocab_size = len(tokenizer.word_index) + 1
52.
53. maxlen = 100
54.
55. X_train = pad_sequences(X_train, padding='post',
    maxlen=maxlen)
56. X_test = pad_sequences(X_test, padding='post',
    maxlen=maxlen)
57. from numpy import array
58. from numpy import asarray
59. from numpy import zeros
60.
```

```
61. embedd_dict= dict()
62. glove_embeddings = open('/gdrive/My Drive/datasets/
    glove.6B.100d.txt', encoding="utf8")
63.
64. for embeddings in glove_embeddings:
65.     embedding_tokens = embeddings.split()
66.     emb_word = embedding_tokens [0]
67.     emb_vector = asarray(   embedding_tokens[1:],
    dtype='float32')
68.     embedd_dict [emb_word] = emb_vector
69.
70. glove_embeddings.close()
71. embedd_mat= zeros((vocab_size, 100))
72. for word, index in tokenizer.word_index.items():
73.     embedding_vector = embedd_dict.get(word)
74.     if embedding_vector is not None:
75.         embedd_mat[index] = embedding_vector
76. embedd_mat.shape
77.
78. embedding_inputs = Input(shape=(maxlen))
79. embedding_layer = Embedding(vocab_size, 100,
    weights=[embedd_mat], trainable=False)(embedding_inputs)
80. flatten_layer = Flatten()(embedding_layer)
81.
82. dense1 = Dense(512, activation='relu')(flatten_layer)
83. do1 = Dropout(0.3)(dense1)
84.
85. dense2 = Dense(512, activation='relu')(do1)
86. do2 = Dropout(0.3)(dense2)
87.
88. dense3 = Dense(512, activation='relu')(do2)
89. do3 = Dropout(0.3)(dense3)
90.
91. output_layer = Dense(y_train.shape[1],
    activation='softmax')(do3)
92. model = Model(embedding_inputs, output_layer)
93.
94. model.compile(optimizer='adam', loss='categorical_
    crossentropy', metrics=['accuracy'])
```

```
95.
96. from tensorflow.keras.utils import plot_model
97. plot_model(model, to_file='model_plot1.png', show_
    shapes=True, show_layer_names=True)
98. history = model.fit(X_train, y_train, batch_size= 128,
    epochs=10, verbose=1, validation_split=0.2)
99.
100.    score = model.evaluate(X_test, y_test, verbose=1)
101.    print(score[0])
102.    print(score[1])
```

Exercise 11.1

Question 1:

This process where ground truth value of the previous output is fed as input to the next timestep, is called _____

    A. Truth Labelling

    B. Input Labelling

    C. Input Forcing

    D. Teacher Forcing

Answer: D

Question 2:

In seq2seq model, the input to the node in the decoder layer is _____

    A. Hidden state from the encoder

    B. Cell state from the encoder

    C. A "start of sentence" tag

    D. All of the above

Answer: D

Question 3:

To end predictions using decoder LSTM in seq2seq, what strategy is adopted?

    A. End sentence if maximum sentence length is achieved

    B. End sentence if "end of sentence" tag is predicted

    C. Both A and B

    D. None of the Above

Answer: C

Exercise 11.2

Using the spa.txt file from *Resources/Datasets*, create a seq2seq model for translating English sentences into Spanish.

Solution:

The solution to this exercise is the same code that you used in Chapter 11 to create a seq2seq model. You only have to replace the "fra.txt" file that contains English to French sentences, with the "Spa.txt" file that contains English to Spanish sentences in order to perform Spanish to French translation.

Exercise 12.1

Question 1:

To convert data into the BERT input format, which function can be used from the BertTokenizer class?

    A. encode

    B. encode_plus

    C. encode_bert

    D. A and B

Answer: D

Question 2:

BERT models are capable of capturing:

    A. Text Similarity

    B. Global Context Information

    C. Local Context Information

    D. All of the above

Answer: D

Question 3:

The transformers library from Hugging Face contains BERT models that cannot be used for:

    A. Image Classification

    B. Text Classification

    C. Both A and B

    D. None of the Above

Answer: A

Exercise 12.2

Using the "ham_spam.csv" file from *Resources/Datasets*, develop a BERT-based sequence classifier.

Solution:

```
1.  import numpy as np
2.
3.  import tensorflow as tf
4.  import tensorflow_hub as hub
5.  import tensorflow_datasets as tfds
6.
7.  import matplotlib.pyplot as plt
8.
9.  print("Version: ", tf.__version__)
10. print("Eager mode: ", tf.executing_eagerly())
11. print("Hub version: ", hub.__version__)
12. print("GPU is", "available" if tf.test.is_gpu_available()
    else "NOT AVAILABLE")
13.
14. from google.colab import drive
15. drive.mount('/gdrive')
16.
17. import pandas as pd
18. import numpy as np
19. import re
20. import nltk
21. from nltk.corpus import stopwords
22.
23. message_dataset= pd.read_csv("/gdrive/My Drive/datasets/
    ham_spam.csv")
24.
25. message_dataset.head()
26. message_dataset.head()
27.
28. def clean_text(doc):
29.
30.     document = remove_tags(doc)
31.
```

```
32.     document = re.sub('[^a-zA-Z]', ' ', document)
33.
34.     document = re.sub(r"\s+[a-zA-Z]\s+", ' ', document)
35.
36.     document = re.sub(r'\s+', ' ', document)
37.
38.     return document
39.
40. TAG_RE = re.compile(r'<[^>]+>')
41.
42. def remove_tags(document):
43.     return TAG_RE.sub('', document)
44.
45. message_dataset["Message"] = message_dataset["Message"].
    apply(clean_text)
46. message_dataset["Category"]  = message_dataset["Category"].
    map({'ham': 1,'spam': 0})
47.
48. ! pip install transformers
49.
50. from sklearn import preprocessing
51. from sklearn.model_selection import train_test_split
52.
53.
54. from transformers import (TFBertForSequenceClassification,
55.                           BertTokenizer)
56.
57. from tqdm import tqdm
58.
59. X = message_dataset["Message"].values
60. y = message_dataset["Category"].values
61.
62. X_train, X_test, y_train, y_test = train_test_split(X, y,
    test_size=0.2, random_state=42)
63.
64. print("Shape of training data: {0}, \nShape of test data:
    {1}".format(X_train.shape, X_test.shape))
65. bert_tokenizer = BertTokenizer.from_pretrained("bert-base-
    cased")
```

```
66. pad_token=0
67. pad_token_segment_id=0
68. max_length= 128
69.
70. def text_to_bert_input(reviews):
71.    input_ids,attention_masks,token_type_ids=[],[],[]
72.
73.    for review in tqdm(reviews,position=0, leave=True):
74.        bert_inputs = bert_tokenizer.encode_plus(review,add_
       special_tokens=True, max_length=max_length, truncation =
       True)
75.
76.        input, token_type = bert_inputs["input_ids"], bert_
       inputs["token_type_ids"]
77.        mask = [1] * len(input)
78.
79.        padding_length = max_length - len(input)
80.
81.        input = input + ([pad_token] * padding_length)
82.        mask = mask + ([0] * padding_length)
83.        token_type  = token_type  + ([pad_token_segment_id] *
       padding_length)
84.
85.        input_ids.append(input)
86.        attention_masks.append(mask)
87.        token_type_ids.append(token_type)
88.
89.    return [np.asarray(input_ids),
90.                np.asarray(attention_masks),
91.                np.asarray(token_type_ids)]
92. X_test_input=text_to_bert_input(X_test)
93. X_train_input=text_to_bert_input(X_train)
94. def convert_to_tensors(input_ids,attention_masks,token_
    type_ids,y):
95.    return {"input_ids": input_ids,
96.             "attention_mask": attention_masks,
97.             "token_type_ids": token_type_ids},y
98.
99.
```

```
100. train_dataset = tf.data.Dataset.from_tensor_slices((X_
     train_input[0],X_train_input[1],X_train_input[2],y_
     train)).map(convert_to_tensors).shuffle(100).batch(32)
101.
102. test_dataset = tf.data.Dataset.from_tensor_slices((X_
     test_input[0],X_test_input[1],X_test_input[2],y_test)).
     map(convert_to_tensors).batch(64)
103. model = TFBertForSequenceClassification.from_
     pretrained("bert-base-cased")
104.
105.
106. optimizer = tf.keras.optimizers.Adam(learning_rate=3e-5,
     epsilon=1e-08)
107. loss = tf.keras.losses.
     SparseCategoricalCrossentropy(from_logits=True)
108. metric = tf.keras.metrics.
     SparseCategoricalAccuracy('accuracy')
109.
110. model.compile(optimizer=optimizer, loss=loss,
     metrics=[metric])
111.
112. model.summary()
113. history = model.fit(train_dataset, epochs=1, validation_
     data=test_dataset)
```

www.ingramcontent.com/pod-product-compliance
Lightning Source LLC
Chambersburg PA
CBHW071232050326
40690CB00011B/2082